OPPORTUNITIES

in

Psychology
Careers

REVISED EDITION

CHARLES M. SUPER, PH.D.
DONALD E. SUPER, PH.D.

New York Chicago San Francisco Lisbon London Madrid Mexico City
Milan New Delhi San Juan Seoul Singapore Sydney Toronto

The *McGraw·Hill* Companies

Library of Congress Cataloging-in-Publication Data

Super, Donald E.
    Opportunities in psychology careers / by Donald E. Super and Charles M. Super.
  —3rd ed.
       p.   cm.
    Includes bibliographical references.
    ISBN-13: 978-0-07-154530-3 (alk. paper)
    ISBN-10: 0-07-154530-1 (alk. paper)
    1. Psychology—Vocational guidance.   I. Title.

BF76.C35   2009
150.23'73—dc22   2008023360

1 2 3 4 5 6 7 8 9 10 11 12 13 14 15 16 17 18 19 20   DOC/DOC 0 9 8

ISBN 978-0-07-154530-3
ISBN 0-07-154530-1

Interior design by Rattray Design

McGraw-Hill books are available at special quantity discounts to use as premiums and sales promotions or for use in corporate training programs. To contact a representative, please visit the Contact Us pages at www.mhprofessional.com.

This book is printed on acid-free paper.

Contents

Counseling psychology. Clinical and abnormal psychology. School psychology. Sports psychology. Emerging specialties, related fields, and interdisciplinary bridges.

Undergraduate education. Graduate preparation. Master's programs. Doctoral programs. Postdoctoral programs. Continuing education. Accredited graduate programs in psychology. Choosing a graduate school. Financing graduate education.

Master's degree holders. Bachelor's degree holders. Rapid growth. Where the jobs are. Diversity in psychology. Compensation for psychologists. Some disadvantages.

Getting started. Getting ahead. Networking. Think tanks, research institutes, and freelance work.

American Psychological Association. Association for Psychological Science. Canadian Psychological Association. American Board of Professional Psychology. Psi Chi. Related associations. State and provincial licensing and certification boards. National Register of Health Service Providers in Psychology.

PREFACE

I SUPPOSE I have no greater interest in and curiosity about people than average. That's only because the average is so high. We are intensely social creatures, and our desire and need to observe, know, wonder, predict, and attempt to influence or control each other is almost as strong as our hunger for food and water. We are all (with the possible exception of a couple of rare forms of psychopathology) driven to spend much of our time trying to figure each other out. So, even though I am a psychologist, I may not be more interested in people than you are. However, I have the great fortune to be able to spend my time and make my living engrossed in this basic human preoccupation.

Not surprisingly, I love what I do. My passion for learning about and interacting with others is carried out in the training clinic at a state university, the place where doctoral students in psychology learn to be therapists and to do psychological assessment. Since psychology is both the science of behavior (I was trained as a researcher) and one of the healing arts (I was trained also to listen, understand, and use my empathy), I have to keep up as well as I can in two separate but related areas. To teach, I have to constantly learn. I learn from reading, observing, and living. Plus, I say without apology, that I learn as much from my students as from any other source. And they learn from me that it's okay and good to be anxious about the work of dealing with fragile and precious people and that they can learn to use themselves and their knowledge to help others.

These days, the most exciting thing I'm learning from and with my students is *neuropsychology*—the study of the brain and how it works. Psychologists have long been the leaders among human scientists and mental health professionals in the development and use of psychological testing to measure mental abilities and emotional characteristics. For the past couple of decades, we've also been able to see, through brain scans or neuroimages, what the brain of a living person looks like and what it's doing when engaged in various tasks. We can't see thoughts, of course, but we can see what parts of the brain "light up" when a person is doing a particular type of thinking. And we can look at people with different diagnoses or normal individuals with different results on our psychological tests and see how their brains function in different ways. Psychologists are working in teams with physicians (neurologists), radiologists, chemists, physicists, computer experts, and others to unravel mysteries about the brain, the body, and human behavior. The results are complex while enlightening—I once read that if the brain were simple to understand, it would be too simple to do the understanding. But it's extraordinary what we're learning.

So far, I can't say that the advances in neuropsychology and neuroimaging have changed how I do and teach psychotherapy and psychological assessment. I do understand my clients in a different way and often am better able to help them see how they developed some of their patterns of perceiving and living. I also have learned that the cognitive therapy that I do results in changes in brain images (brain chemistry) that are similar to what happens when the person takes some of the valuable new medications for depression. But for now, I can enjoy the pure science of it all, because whatever I learn about people and how they think and how they deal with their emotions and relate to other people is part of what I'm supposed to do in my job. That's one of the loveliest parts of what I do—anything I read, see, experience, hear, talk about with others, feel, or find inside myself can become part of my work, if I spend the time to reflect on it and develop my understanding. Even my own weaknesses provide valuable information (and no, I haven't gotten rid of all my own weaknesses and flaws).

Psychology at its best is both the collecting of information and the application of careful methodology and reason to understand what that information means. I often describe psychology as the most skeptical of all the mental health disciplines, and I like that about it. The bookshelves are filled with self-help guides, and claims about improving the human condition are spread throughout numerous sections of bookstores. Psychologists (and others with a scientific approach to human problems and behavior) have helped us and will continue to help us sort through these claims and refine our thinking about how to be human and how to improve the human condition.

So, one of the promises that psychology holds for you if you study it and work with it is a different understanding of yourself, the people you meet, and human nature. I could have said "a better understanding," and that would probably be true, but I think the more honest claim is that you will come to understand people differently—more richly, complexly, and deeply. But you're likely also to become more aware of what you don't know and to doubt the ways you've typically come to categorize and predict and influence others. (To be honest, there are dogmatic and arrogant psychologists who think they know it all. I myself find the whole endeavor profoundly humbling, while enlightening.) If your teachers are successful, you'll grow in both knowledge and doubt—and in acceptance of yourself and others. That doesn't mean you'll lose your ability to believe and judge and be moral, but your morality is likely to become richer and more complex, too. I know I'm different as a person because I chose this field.

All this adds up to a mixed bag of values that comes out of studying psychology and practicing psychology. Whether you simply take psychology courses, major in it, or do advanced work toward a master's degree or a doctorate, you will increase your knowledge, change your way of looking at and thinking about yourself and others, and simultaneously develop more questions, more doubts, and a healthy skepticism. If you're okay with ambiguity and are willing to put at risk any feeling you might have in the security of your judgments, go for it. You'll never be bored.

Dan Matthews, Ph.D.
Director, Department of Psychology Clinic
University of New Mexico
Albuquerque, New Mexico

1

An Overview of Psychology

SOME PROFESSIONS ARE fairly easy to understand. For instance, most of us can probably say with confidence that we know what a defense attorney does or that we understand the work of a pharmacist. Other professions are more difficult to pinpoint. It is likely that far fewer people can describe the work of an acoustical mechanic—a person who installs sound-absorbing ceiling and wall panels in buildings.

So where does psychology fall on this scale of understanding? Many people think they know what a psychologist is and believe they understand the profession, but many others are uncertain of the facts about psychology and the many varieties of work that it includes.

In today's society, more people than ever have encountered psychologists in different settings, whether in school, industry, or the armed forces. They may see psychologists as mental testers or as the helpful people in the guidance or human resources office who always had time to listen to what you thought you wanted to do.

Any one of these pictures of a psychologist is good as far as it goes, but it does not go very far.

Three Psychologies

There are three different ways of looking at what psychology is. It is an *academic discipline*, a body of knowledge with themes of method and content that tie together disparate parts. The knowledge is organized and synthesized into theories and "schools of thought" for communication among members of the scientific community and for transmittal to students and other interested parties. Thus psychologists may be teachers and writers.

The way psychology's knowledge is expanded through various methods of structured inquiry makes psychology a *science*. The scientist fashions questions and guidelines for finding answers to those questions. Many psychologists spend their time in a laboratory as part of a research team.

Psychology is also a *profession*, an organized way of using the academic and scientific knowledge for the betterment of individuals and groups of individuals. In this sense, professional psychologists practice psychotherapy and advise business managers, plan mental health services, find effective ways to display computerized information, and diagnose children's problems in school.

No one psychologist, of course, carries out all the activities of each aspect of psychology, and the variety of combinations that people choose for their careers is part of what makes understanding the nature of psychology seem complicated at first. It is also true that some aspects of psychology are much more familiar to nonpsychologists than are others, and some of the familiar roles appear similar to roles in other occupations.

For example, it is common for people to confuse psychologists and psychiatrists. Psychologists differ from psychiatrists partly in the content of their training and partly in the work they generally do. The differences in their training are best summed up by the different academic degrees each holds. The psychiatrist earns the degree of doctor of medicine (M.D.), studying the biological sciences that are basic to the profession of medicine and the techniques of medical practice. More knowledge of psychiatry is acquired later in practical training and related study.

The fully trained psychologist, on the other hand, earns the degree of doctor of philosophy (Ph.D.), psychology (Psy.D.), or education (Ed.D.). The Ph.D. is still the most common higher degree. The psychologist studies the biological and social sciences related to psychology and specializes in the science of psychology as a graduate student. Preparation for an applied field may include the study of relevant professional problems and methods and further practical training after the doctorate. This means that, like the physician who later specializes in psychiatry, the psychologist has been trained in the principles and techniques of a special field of knowledge and its supporting fields. It also means that, unlike the psychiatrist, the psychologist has been trained primarily in the behavioral sciences. Psychologists also are trained in research methods that enable them to add to their store of knowledge.

Psychology is both a science and a profession. As a science, psychology is the study of how people perceive, think, feel, and act; as a profession, it is concerned with predicting how people will act, helping people to modify their behavior, and helping organizations, communities, and societies change. So a psychologist, may spend time in research, adding to our knowledge of behavior and developing new ways of understanding behavior, or helping people and institutions change their behavior, structure, or functions. Or the psychologist may spend more time working with people, studying them by examining records of what they have done or talking with them to help them modify their behavior, change the methods of their organizations, or put their resources to better use.

Many psychologists work with people and conduct research. Working with people provides firsthand knowledge of the important problems to be studied and often leads to improved ways to study them. There is a better chance that what is learned through research will be used if the researcher also works with people. For these reasons, university programs for the professional preparation of psychologists who will work with people include a good deal of emphasis on research.

Many psychologists become scientists rather than practitioners. In this respect they are like neuroscientists, bacteriologists, and other natural scientists whose research results are used by physicians in the treatment of illnesses, or like sociologists, economists, and other social scientists, whose research knowledge is used in government, industry, and education. Many other psychologists become practitioners, putting into practice the knowledge that they and their pure-scientist colleagues accumulate.

A Brief Look at Psychology Specialties

The specialties include clinical psychology, industrial-organizational psychology, and school psychology. In some respects, clinical psychologists resemble psychiatrists because they apply their knowledge of psychological principles and methods to the diagnosis and treatment of mental disorders. The main concern of industrial-organizational psychologists is the study and improvement of personnel practices in industry and government. School psychologists use their knowledge to help teachers understand and work more effectively with their students. They also help children and parents make better adjustments to school and life in general.

In all three specialties the psychologist works in a field that is more social than biological because the problems of personal adjustment are primarily problems of interpersonal or human relations. The clinical psychologist and the psychiatrist do have common ground in the problems of mental health, along with the psychiatric social worker and the psychiatric nurse. However, the psychiatrist makes a distinctive medical contribution to study and treatment, and often there is a focus on illness and healing. The psychologist makes a distinctive sociopsychological contribution, with an emphasis on changing behavior.

Whatever their specialty, psychologists are not the only practitioners. Behavioral scientists, who are specialists in developmental psychology, personality theory, social psychology, educational psychology, and experimental psychology, find that their understanding of human behavior and the methods that they bring to bear upon its study results in their becoming increasingly involved in practice.

Most often, these specialists apply their knowledge to the behavior of normal people functioning in everyday circumstances, rather than people with serious problems. Experimental psychologists find themselves involved in engineering problems in industry or in medical problems in space exploration. Educational and developmental psychologists are drawn into designing and evaluating new methods of teaching the handicapped, the normal, and the gifted. Social psychologists help plan and evaluate the outcome of government policies or political campaigns. Personality theorists may participate in any of these projects. A more in-depth look at the various specializations is provided in Chapter 2.

Questions in Psychology

It may be helpful to consider some of the kinds of problems that psychologists work on. A discussion of the scientific questions studied by psychologists follows, after which some of the more practical problems psychologists work on are reviewed. The distinction between the scientific and the practical, while convenient, is actually difficult to make and to justify. For example, the problem of the localization of brain functions is of interest not only for an understanding of human intellectual functioning but also because it has practical importance in the rehabilitation of brain-injured people. Similarly, the practical use of tests for predicting educational or vocational success throws theoretical light on the structure of mental abilities by showing how differential aptitudes are related to significant social behavior.

Psychology as a Science

About one-fifth of America's psychologists are employed primarily in research. Whether their work is more aptly called basic or applied is often difficult to decide, as the examples given here will make clear. Many psychologists employed primarily in teaching or in practice spend some time in the study of psychological problems or issues, although the questions asked, the methods used, and the types of data collected and analyzed vary widely.

Psychology of Memory

The psychology of memory, especially for highly emotional and painful events, has long held a special interest for psychologists. A primary focus of Freud's early work, for example, was to recover adult patients' repressed memories of traumatic experiences, on the theory that these experiences held the key to patients' current suffering. His later conclusion that many of the memories were actually fantasies, or unfulfilled wishes related to infantile sexuality that were not permitted into the stream of normal consciousness, was one origin of his theory of neurotic disorders. Modern findings about the frequency of child sexual abuse has raised the question for many psychologists of whether Freud was too quick to call these stories fantasies rather than painful memories struggling to be recalled. Some therapists have therefore been careful to consider all such memories by patients as potentially true, unless there is very good reason to think they were fabricated or imagined.

The question of accuracy in memory is of great importance when there are allegations of sexual abuse of children. More than twenty thousand children testify each year in abuse trials, and their testimony is usually considered to be truthful and accurate unless proven otherwise. But research by psychologists Maggie Bruck of Johns Hopkins Hospital and Stephen Ceci of Cornell University has called into question even this assumption about memory. They found that persistent, repeated questioning on a particular topic over a period of several weeks can lead young children (under six years old) to remember events that never took place. Often child victims of suspected abuse are repeatedly asked about alleged events by a parent, the police, and caseworkers. But a child in the study by Ceci and his colleagues, for example, who had never been to the hospital, recounted a detailed, if somewhat disjointed, story about his visit to the hospital after being questioned about it once a week for eleven consecutive weeks.

It seems that children normally construct their memories in part from what they hear from adults about their own past experiences.

While these findings about the way memory works in children makes interesting science, it also makes much more difficult the job of psychologists and others who have the responsibility of investigating questions of abuse and protecting the children involved, as well as respecting the rights of the accused. Ceci and Bruck, among others, have made suggestions about improving the methods used in such investigations in order to minimize the possibility of error.

Psychology of Learning

Psychologists have long been interested in the physiological basis of the way humans learn. It was this interest that prompted much of the well-known research on rats in mazes, some of which tried to determine how memories are formed in the neurons and chemicals of the brain. Another line of investigation that led to a new technique for promoting certain kinds of learning is biofeedback, in which the subject learns to exert deliberate control over bodily functions that were earlier thought to be uncontrollable. The principle is a simple one: the behavior to be influenced—for example, the heart rate—is monitored by an electronic device. A second piece of apparatus signals by a light or a sound when the heart is going faster or slower than a predetermined rate. The subject or patient can then learn to exercise some control over the heart rate in response to the signal.

Biofeedback has helped people learn how to influence their own heart rate, blood pressure, and even the brain waves associated with different states of consciousness. Research on biofeedback illustrates both the coherence of psychology across specialties and the interplay between pure and applied science in psychology. The techniques of biofeedback were developed by psychologists with backgrounds in both physiological and experimental psychology and were quickly recognized by personality and clinical psychologists, physicians, and others as potentially useful in the treatment of some kinds of psychosomatic problems and psychological anxieties.

In recent years, biofeedback has been incorporated into therapy for more traditional medical problems involving irregularities of the heartbeat, gastric ulcers, asthma, and epilepsy. The results of this work are posing major new questions to other psychologists about theories of learning, psychophysiology, personality, and mental functioning.

Structure of Mental Ability

Another question faced by psychologists concerns the structure of mental ability. Specifically, is there such a thing as general intelligence, or is intelligence actually made up of a number of special abilities? Early theory described a number of distinct mental faculties, but the work of French psychologist Alfred Binet led to the development of intelligence tests and the abandonment of the idea of separate faculties of mind. Other psychologists, in particular the late Dr. L. L. Thurston of the University of Chicago, used improved tests, experimental designs, and statistical methods to break general intelligence into a number of primary mental abilities. The number of primary mental abilities continues to increase with improved methods.

The nature and nurture of intelligence continues to attract psychological researchers. Howard Gardner of Harvard University has organized evidence that there are seven "intelligences," not only the logical and linguistic skills of traditional tests, but also musical intelligence, spatial intelligence, bodily kinesthetic intelligence, the capacity to know oneself, and the ability to understand others. In presenting his theory of multiple intelligences, Gardner draws on research from neuropsychology, developmental psychology, and metric psychology, as well as related fields in cognitive science and anthropology.

It has often been assumed that tested intelligence of a high level is genius. But research by J. P. Guilford of the University of Southern California, Paul Torrance of the University of Georgia, and Jacob W. Getzels and Philip W. Jackson of the University of Chicago found that genius consists of more than a higher level of intelligence as measured by standardized tests. Real genius also requires abilities and traits that enable the individual to see the possibility of combining ideas or things in new ways and thus come up with novel solutions to problems or new uses for old materials.

Because old ideas of group or racial superiority involve assumptions about the general abilities of certain peoples, they provide a research base for psychologists who have used their knowledge and methods to study such claims. They are often joined in this work by anthropologists and sociologists. Dr. Otto Kleinberg, a psychologist who has pursued a distinguished career both at Columbia University and at the Sorbonne in Paris, compared the tested intelligence of African-Americans who remained in the South with that of African-Americans who migrated to the North. He collected substantial evidence to show that differences in environment, rather than in heredity, are the important factors underlying the differences between the intelligence test scores of African-Americans and Caucasians. Some aspects of these findings were questioned by Dr. Arthur Jensen of the University of California at Berkeley. He argued that possible racial differences in mental functioning (which may, in fact, sometimes favor Caucasians and sometimes African-Americans) should be given intensive study. Most psychologists do not agree with his interpretations, but controversy continues over the cultural, social, nutritional, and medical influences on intellectual development and performance, unfortunately often fed by people who generate more controversy than enlightenment.

The debate is not exclusive to the world of academia, however. Because of the controversy over the appropriate use of intelligence tests with persons from minority backgrounds, a legal suit was brought in California to prevent IQ tests from being used in the school placement of African-American children. Psychologists were involved in both sides of the legal argument, which eventually resulted in a court injunction against using IQ data to place minority children in special education classes.

Development of Morality

Why do some people develop a strong sense of conscience while others are less sensitive to right and wrong? Why are some people naturally more helpful than others? Why do some laugh at another person's mishap while others rush to help those in trouble? These questions have long interested psychologists, just as they have challenged philosophers, sociologists, and many others.

To answer such questions, personality psychologists have studied how different types of families teach morality and social values; developmental psychologists have investigated how children of different ages think about moral questions and how they respond to the needs of others; and social psychologists have collected and analyzed data on how group pressures and situational factors affect moral behavior. Everyday life makes it obvious that no one has yet learned how to make everyone perfect, but useful ideas have been developed about how to encourage the learning of constructive, helpful behavior.

This continues to be a lively field of research, especially as psychologists, like many other citizens, respond to what they see as ethical problems related to war, terrorism, violent crime, deceitful behavior in business and politics, and other ills that are as numerous today as they were in ancient times.

In recent years, this research has been employed in preventive programs for school-age children. A program in New Haven, Connecticut, combines principles developed in cognitive psychology, child development, and person-centered therapy to promote social competence through a school-based program. Educational and community psychologists in a number of cities are working on similar programs to help children acquire the social and behavioral skills that may help them avoid the dangers of drug abuse, teenage pregnancy, and AIDS as well as encourage constructive activity for the benefit of themselves and their communities.

Psychology as a Profession

Half of the psychologists working in the United States and Canada are employed primarily in professional activities, putting psychological knowledge to work in everyday life. Psychologists often are thought of as test specialists, and many of them are. One of the largest testing organizations is the Educational Testing Service, with headquarters in Princeton, New Jersey, and locations around the world. Its staff members develop tests that aid in the selection and guidance of students in college and various professional schools. They also conduct research in the development of new types of tests for educational selection and evaluation.

The armed forces of the United States and Canada, the U.S. Office of Personnel Management, the Canadian Civil Service Commission, and many business and industrial organizations employ similar staffs of psychologists working on problems of testing and related procedures for personnel selection and classification. Advances in computer-based testing allow for more individualized and appropriate test questions and more convenient scheduling, and they offer more in-depth insights into test-takers than conventional exams.

Assessment, Counseling, and Testing

Psychologists are also commonly involved in assessment and counseling, in which they work with students or adult clients to help them achieve better self-understanding, to make wise plans, and to take steps toward self-fulfillment in college, at work, at home, and in the use of leisure time.

Psychologists are also concerned with the diagnosis and modification of behavior, as well as emotional and intellectual disorders. Those working in schools, psychological clinics, mental health clinics, and hospitals study children and adults by means of tests, play techniques, and interviews to better understand their behavior. They also help these people to modify their behavior by using various techniques of play, discussion, and work.

This work is generally carried out with careful planning in appropriately designed institutions, but more and more psychologists are called to help in unusual crises. For example, in 1987 a major airplane crash in Detroit killed 153 people. A vice president of the airline asked Dr. James Butcher of the University of Minnesota to organize immediate mental health counseling for employees and victims' families. In the next ten days, approximately twelve hundred people in six cities around the country were helped with the problems of depression, traumatic loss, guilt, and anger. Individually and in groups, in offices, airport crew lounges, and over the telephone, psychologists began a course of work that dealt with the tragedy in an immediate and effective way in an unusual collaboration between the corporate and academic communities.

Following the 1995 Oklahoma City bombing, President Bill Clinton asked aides to consult with child-care specialists and psychologists about how to talk with children about the tragedy. Three days after the bombing, President and Mrs. Clinton met with children of federal employees in a live nationwide television and radio broadcast, where they addressed the children's concerns about the bombing.

Psychologists also employ psychological testing, which uses samples of behavior in order to infer generalizations about an individual subject. This involves observations over time of an individual performing tasks that have usually been prescribed beforehand. These responses are often compiled into statistical tables that allow the evaluator to compare the behavior of the individual being tested to the responses of a control group.

For example, scientists and health officials are concerned about the possibility that exposure to toxins released in the collapse of the World Trade Center may have negative effects on fetal development. To study this question, a children's environmental health center is currently analyzing children whose mothers were pregnant during the collapse of the World Trade Center and were living or working near the towers. The children are assessed using psychological testing every year, and their mothers are interviewed every six months. The purpose of the study is to determine whether there is significant difference in development and health progression of children whose mothers were exposed versus those who were not.

Training and Group Processes

Psychologists help people not only through counseling and clinical work but also through the analysis and improvement of group procedures, interpersonal relations, and organizational functioning. For example, Dr. Alfred Marrow, textile corporation president and industrial psychologist, became interested in what effects would occur if workers discussed plans for new company policies before they are made as opposed to setting policies and then telling workers about them. He asked psychologists of the Research Center for Group Dynamics at the University of Michigan to conduct an experiment in one of his plants in order to test these two methods of decision making. The experiment showed more complete acceptance of policy changes and more cooperation when decision making was preceded by worker discussion of facts and issues. Many consulting and some staff psychologists now help industry use these methods.

The improvement of training or educational methods is an important area of applied psychology. Many city school systems and universities have bureaus of educational research that employ educational psychologists. These people work on problems of instructional methods, the organization of subject matter, and the evaluation of instruction.

When training problems arise—whether in schools, colleges, businesses, industry, government, or the armed forces—they may be solved by nonpsychologist practitioners, such as teachers, human resources staff, and others on the basis of general psychological knowledge or experience. On the other hand, they may be solved with the assistance of psychologists who are more expert in the psychology of learning and more experienced in designing methods of ascertaining how well methods actually work.

Not only do psychologists study, devise, and improve methods of training, they also work on methods of doing the work itself. Engineering psychologists work on such problems as the flow of work and arrangement of the work area, the sequence of movements and processes, and the design of the machine in relation to the person who must operate it. Because of their knowledge of human abilities and behavior, combined with training in experimental methods, psychologists are in a position to make a special contribution to adapting the machine to the worker, as well as to selecting the right person for the machine.

How individuals learn to work in groups has long been a topic of applied psychological research. As with many other topics in psychology, this one was given a strong start by the needs of the military during World War II. The effective team functioning of bomber crews under combat conditions was often critical to their success and survival. In order to know better how to train these crews, their interactions during training and combat were studied to ascertain the characteristics of effective and ineffective groups, the characteristics and behavior of the members of each of these types of groups, and the factors that make for the emergence and exercise of successful leadership. The eventual success of this work significantly facilitated the training of air crews and saved many lives of crewmembers. These results are still in use. One example is studies conducted at the Naval Training Systems Center that focus on decision making under conditions of extreme stress.

Survey Techniques

The techniques of market research and public opinion polling are further examples of the application of psychological methods. Many psychologists are employed by consulting organizations, advertising agencies, and survey centers that are conducting studies of what the consumer wants and of what the public thinks about various issues. Designing questions that will elicit meaningful answers, conducting surveys in ways that will get cooperation and a true sample of the public, and interpreting findings are activities that call for psychological training and skill.

For example, it has been shown that opinion pollsters who use interview methods are more likely to get honest responses if they are on the same social level and of the same race as the person they are interviewing.

Psychology as an Academic Pursuit and Instructional Field

Many psychologists—about one-fifth of them—are primarily teachers. A generation ago, this was true of more than half of America's psychologists, but research organizations and practice have absorbed the increasing numbers of young people who are entering the profession. Although psychology is increasingly being introduced as a subject of study in high schools, the great majority of teaching psychologists are employed in colleges and universities.

In high schools, community colleges, and liberal arts colleges, psychology instructors are concerned largely with the general educational value of psychology for all students, in the belief that a better understanding of human behavior will be beneficial to everyone. In professional schools, psychology professors are concerned with helping students, physicians, social workers, engineers, librarians, teachers, businesspeople, and others understand and master appropriate psychological principles and techniques. In graduate schools, psychology professors are concerned with the training of other psychologists for teaching, research, and professional applications or practice. Emphasis varies from one graduate school to another and even from one program to another in the same psychology department, such as from a physiological program to an organizational program.

Psychology and the Public Debate

The results of psychological research have proven valuable in public debates and policy making in legislatures, executive offices, courtrooms, school boards, and other arenas, where competing ideas about social reality and what to do about it come together. The U.S. Department of Health and Human Services and Health Canada continually work toward establishing and updating federal policies for children and families, as well as treating illnesses and psychological disorders.

The Department of Health and Human Services includes more than three hundred programs. Following are some examples of the areas in which psychological research is used:

- Health and social science research
- Head Start (preschool education and services)
- Preventing child abuse and domestic violence
- Substance abuse treatment and prevention
- Services for older citizens
- Health services for Native Americans
- Improving maternal and infant health

One of these areas, the Head Start program, has been cited as a proven way to provide children with the necessary foundation for long-term success. The program was initiated in part because of the concerns of psychologists and educators in the 1960s who provided the experimental models on which it was based. This work has demonstrated the educational, social, health, and economic benefits of such programs so effectively that Head Start now enjoys the strong support of legislators and citizens from all political parties and across nearly all branches of government.

The National Institutes of Health is at the forefront of medical and behavioral research in the United States. Its mission is science in pursuit of fundamental knowledge about the nature and behavior of living systems and the application of that knowledge to extend healthy life and reduce the burdens of illness and disability. In particular, the National Institute of Mental Health (NIMH) is the world's largest scientific organization dedicated to research focused on the understanding, treatment, and prevention of mental disorders and the promotion of mental health.

The NIMH conducts research in the following areas of interest to psychologists:

- Anxiety disorders
- Attention deficit hyperactivity disorder (ADHD, ADD)
- Autism spectrum disorders (pervasive developmental disorders)
- Bipolar disorders (manic-depressive disorders)
- Borderline personality disorder
- Depression
- Eating disorders
- Obsessive-compulsive disorder
- Panic disorder
- Post-traumatic stress disorder
- Schizophrenia
- Social anxiety disorder

The topics of public debate addressed by psychological and behavioral research are innumerable. They include issues such as recycling used materials; discrimination in the workplace; promoting healthy behaviors, especially for those at high risk; the proper role of eyewitness testimony; the alleged preventive effects of capital punishment; as well as the more traditional topics of mental health and educational reform.

The recent growth of applying research results to policy matters reflects several trends. One is simply the accumulation of a much larger body of knowledge than was available in previous decades. This in turn is partly the result of the growing number of psychologists and other behavioral scientists who have been trained in research. In addition, a number of people and organizations, such as the American Psychological Association, have made extensive efforts to bring this knowledge to the attention of relevant groups of decision makers. Finally, the trend probably also reflects the increasing sophistication of the American public and its representatives with regard to the possibility of understanding human behavior through scientific research.

Psychology's Place in Society

By now, it should be clear that psychology has an important place in society. It has a place wherever there are people; since wherever there are people, there are problems of organization, performance, and adjustment. Wherever there are people, there are problems stemming from how to live and work together, how to learn or how to function, and how to live with oneself.

Increased awareness of these problems generally means increased willingness to provide funds for understanding and treating them.

To solve all of these problems, psychologists can contribute relevant principles for the guidance of policy or for decision making; techniques of investigation to get a better understanding of the problem or for the evaluation of methods and results; and assistance in devising and trying out solutions.

Who Should Enter the Profession?

So far, you have seen something of the nature of the field of psychology and the psychologist's work. In the following chapters, we will look further into the areas of specialization, the necessary education and training, the job prospects and compensation, and how to plan a career. First, however, let's take a moment to discuss what sort of person should enter this field.

To be fully trained as a psychologist, you must have a doctorate degree, and to be employable as a technician in psychology, a master's degree is highly desirable. This means that you should have at least enough academic ability to be capable of graduate study at a university. If you aspire to a position of leadership, you should be capable of the advanced study and research necessary for a Ph.D., Psy.D., or Ed.D. degree.

Psychology is a scientific profession devoted to the study of human behavior and the improvement of human adjustment, which means that the student of psychology should believe that knowledge is important, that time and energy should be spent in finding out what is true, and that principles and facts should be put to work in the interest of human welfare. It means that the student should consider knowledge and welfare ultimately more important than one's own material well-being, prestige, or aesthetic values; although these, too, have their proper place in one's life.

Psychology involves working carefully and precisely with large numbers of detailed observations concerning human or animal behavior, bringing together and understanding these data by statistical or other methods, reading widely and deeply in theoretical and applied subjects, and dealing with people as colleagues, clients, subjects, and students. The extent to which a given psychologist does each of these things depends partly on his or her specialty and partly on the kind of institution or organization in which he or she carries on the work of his or her special field.

All psychologists need to be interested in the careful study of behavior and in collecting, organizing, and understanding data concerned with behavior. All need scholarly interests and work habits. Interest in working with people may vary considerably, for in some specialties the psychologist may deal only indirectly with people other than professional colleagues or students. In other specialties, the psychologist works closely with people of varied backgrounds and personal characteristics.

The personality requirements of psychology are to some extent suggested by the interest requirements. Psychologists need patience and persistence in working with varied and complex data, coupled with the ability to work toward remote goals that are often difficult to attain. If they are employed in the applied or professional specialties, they need to be tolerant of individual differences and personality deviations in others. In clinical, counseling, and especially school psychology, a wholesome personal adjustment and a genuine acceptance of and interest in others are crucial personality requirements.

2

SPECIALIZATIONS IN PSYCHOLOGY

As MENTIONED EARLIER, psychology is unusual in that it is both a science and a profession. Some psychologists are primarily scientists, engaged in research work and perhaps in related administrative and teaching activities. Others are primarily practitioners, engaged in the application of psychology to practical problems of education, business, industry, health, welfare, and everyday living. Although many scientists also apply their knowledge of principles and methods and many practitioners carry on research, psychologists generally can be characterized according to one of these functions.

Moreover, there is further specialization within the field of psychology just as there is within the fields of physics and medicine. Just as the science of physics can be divided into specialties, such as astrophysics and nuclear physics, so the science of psychology can be divided into specialties, such as experimental psychology, physiological psychology, developmental psychology, personality psychology, social psychology, abnormal psychology, and psychometrics or measurement. Just as the profession of medicine is divided into specialties, such as pediatrics and internal medicine, so the profession of psychology is divided into specialties, such as clinical, counseling, school, engineering, industrial-organizational, and applied social psychology (market research, propaganda, advertising, public opinion, morale, and group dynamics).

The following list represents the various specialized areas of psychology that are recognized by the American Psychological Association (APA).

Addictions
Adult development
Advertising
Aging
Applied experimental psychology
Arts
Assessment
Behavior analysis
Child, youth, and family services
Children
Clinical child psychology
Clinical psychology
Community psychology
Comparative psychology
Conflict resolution
Consulting psychology
Consumer psychology
Counseling psychology
Criminal justice

Developmental disabilities
Developmental psychology
Disability
Eating disorders
Education
Engineering
Environmental psychology
Ergonomics
Ethnic minorities
Evaluation
Exercise
Experimental analysis of behavior
Experimental psychology
Family issues
Forensic psychology
General psychology
Group psychology
Health psychology
History of psychology
Human factors
Human resources
Humanistic psychology
Hypnosis
Independent practice
Industrial and organizational psychology
International psychology
Law and psychology
Lesbian, gay, and bisexual issues
Measurement psychology
Media

Men and masculinity
Mental retardation
Military psychology
Neuropsychology
Neuroscience
Peace
Pediatric psychology
Perception
Personality
Pharmacotherapy
Philosophical psychology
Physiology
Police and public safety
Population psychology
Psychoanalysis
Psychopharmacology
Psychotherapy
Public service
Rehabilitation
Religion
School psychology
Social policy issues
Social psychology
Spirituality
Sport psychology
State association affairs
Statistics
Substance abuse
Teaching
Testing

Theoretical psychology
Therapy
Trauma
Veterans affairs
Vocational psychology
Women

In this chapter we discuss more than a dozen of these fields in detail to give you an idea of the duties, qualifications, places of employment, and prospects for both doctorate- and master's-level psychologists in each of these specialties. For more information on specializations, as well as career information for psychology students, visit the APA website at www.apa.org.

Although the focus of this chapter is on specialties within psychology, don't assume this means that psychology is a field of specialties differing from each other and lacking common ground. On the contrary, the American Psychological Association's Education and Training Board, other such committees, and most departments of psychology emphasize the importance of a firm grounding in the field of general psychology. The object here is to underline the unity of psychology while pointing out its specialized fields of study and practice.

It is also helpful to note that the particular divisions of psychology used as subfields are to some extent arbitrary and are the outcome of historical, rather than purely logical, factors. Like psychology as a whole, the subfields are constantly growing and changing, sometimes redefining themselves or combining so closely with other trends as to become something new. The specialties listed here, however, are commonly recognized ones at present and serve as a good orientation to the larger profession.

Experimental and Physiological Psychology

Experimental and physiological psychology were once the dominant areas of specialization in many psychology departments. However, with the growth of health service provider specialties and other fields such as social and developmental psychology, their role has changed in several ways.

While the experimental method remains an important tool in all areas of psychological science, the growth of experimental psychology as a subfield—with its focus on sensation, perception, and learning—has not kept pace with some of the other fields. This is partly because some of the newer areas also depend on other approaches to the collection and analysis of data (for example, one cannot easily conduct experiments on long-term questions about personality development in children).

On the other hand, physiological psychology, now more commonly called *neuropsychology* or *cognitive neuroscience*, has advanced dramatically as it draws on and contributes to new techniques and discoveries in biology, neurology, and endocrinology. The experimental method remains at the core of this field, and the two areas—experimental and physiological—are now often considered to be one.

Experimental Psychology

This specialty is concerned with the processes of sensation, perception, learning, and motivation. It studies problems of seeing, hearing, feeling, perceiving, learning, and wanting. These can best be studied in a laboratory situation and are basic to an understanding of the processes of knowing, thinking, judging, and problem solving. Experiments in the field of perception and cognition have made important contributions to both theory and practice in psychology.

The work of experimental psychologists may involve studying how people attend to and use different kinds of visual and auditory information as well as how this processing of information is affected by what they are looking or listening for. For example, they may study the differences in thinking between novices and masters in chess; the ways that rats learn to depend on their own efforts or on the efforts of others in getting food from a vending apparatus; the effect of the judgments of others on an individual's own judgment of the size of an object; or the effects of two different arrangements of aircraft controls on pilot performance.

The training of experimental psychologists emphasizes under-graduate preparation in mathematics and the natural sciences, including physics, chemistry, and physiology. In graduate school, the stress is on experimental methods, sense organ functions, analysis of the learning process, and on the theories related to these. Students spend much time designing and conducting experiments as well as in constructing or becoming familiar with the required laboratory apparatus.

Some preparation in developmental, educational, abnormal, cognitive, or industrial-organizational psychology or in personality theory usually is included. This is done to increase the range of problem areas in which the experimental psychologist may conduct research as well as to prepare the psychologist to teach the variety of courses usually required of instructors in colleges and universities.

A Ph.D. is generally the minimum requirement for a career in experimental psychology except in some lower-level positions, and these positions usually are held by persons working toward their doctorates.

Physiological Psychology

Physiological psychology is the study of how the physiology and anatomy of the brain, its neural network, and the hormonal system it interacts with control behavior—from eating and sex to reading and solving puzzles and caring about other people. Most of this work is carried out on animals, usually rats, cats, and monkeys. (Thus, some of this work is called *comparative psychology*, where the results from different species can be compared.) Occasionally, however, an accident in which a person's nervous system is damaged in a certain way, or an unusual case requiring neurosurgery, will stimulate an important discovery in human physiological psychology.

Research on brain function has always involved psychologists with specialists in such other fields as neurology, pharmacology, endocrinology, biology, and ethology. All of these are rapidly growing fields, and physiological psychologists contribute by working on issues that tie them together. Indeed, subspecialties now can be identified in neuropsychology, psychopharmacology, and other hybrid areas.

Much of the early work in physiological psychology focused on the control of eating and drinking behavior in dogs and cats and added to general knowledge of how the nervous system senses the body's needs and directs their fulfillment. Recent work is in areas more obviously psychological, such as how the nervous systems of different species of animals facilitate certain kinds of learning that are particularly relevant for their survival, or exactly what the brain does as it constructs ideas from patches of black ink on white paper. Another rapidly growing area is called *psychoneuroendocrinology*, where researchers study the interactions of personality, stress, bodily functions, and disease. The techniques of such research range from surgery to carefully controlled environments, from simple observation to elegantly designed experiments.

The graduate training of a physiological psychologist naturally emphasizes the study of neuroanatomy, neurochemistry, animal behavior, and laboratory techniques. Students generally work on their research with assistance from one or two professors. A fortunate undergraduate may have the opportunity to help in a professor's research, but more often his or her preparation consists of course work in biology and chemistry, preferably also physics and electronics, and supplementing with courses in experimental psychology, personality theory, learning, and motivation.

The divisions of physiological, comparative, and experimental psychology are some of the fastest growing areas. A recent survey suggests that more than two-thirds of psychologists in these specializations are employed in colleges and universities, where they teach and conduct research. Some experimental and physiological psychologists work for federal, state, or foundation research projects. Applied experimental psychologists work in the field of engineering psychology in universities and consulting organizations that have military or industrial contracts or in government or industrial organizations.

Engineering Psychology

Most engineering psychologists work in industry, generally as engineering or "human factors" psychologists, but many are employed by the government. The navy employs them in research positions in the Office of Naval Research and in other such installations; the air force employs a number who work on the design of equipment appropriate to human capacities.

Business and industry as well as the military have benefited from recognition of what applied experimental psychology can contribute to the design and use of equipment through the "human factors" approach. It is not only military and spacecraft that present problems of the arrangement and illumination of instruments and control panels but also commercial aircraft, automobiles, and computers; all have problems of access and control. In the case of computers, for example, there are questions of brightness and contrast in the displays of monitors. What characteristics cause operator fatigue problems, and what kind of lighting best combines visibility with restfulness? The arrangement of the different types of office machines for their most effective use in transcription, reproduction, and distribution has been another topic of applied research by human factors psychologists. They sometimes team with personnel and organizational psychologists who focus more on individuals and groups than on equipment.

There are consulting firms that specialize in contract work of this type, often coordinating with manufacturers' staff psychologists. To the surprise of some experimental psychologists, applied experimental or engineering psychology became, during the two decades following World War II, a high-demand field, but there is no longer a major shortage of qualified persons, due to lessened demand in industry, government, and universities. Only a small percentage of psychologists identify themselves as engineering psychologists.

Engineering psychology is now a distinct field, with preparation similar to that of experimental psychology but stressing industrial and military equipment and methods—human factors applications. Training usually calls for attaining a Ph.D., with work in experimental psychology supplemented by organizational and personnel psychology.

Although not numerous, engineering and human factors psychologists have developed considerable esprit de corps. In some metropolitan areas, they meet regularly for the exchange of information about research problems, methods, and applications.

Developmental Psychology

This field of psychology often is divided into the special areas of infant, child, adolescent, adult, and geriatric psychology (gerontology). These specialties are increasingly linked together as life-span developmental psychology. The field is concerned with growth and development from the beginning of life until death; because of the importance of the formative years, it generally has concentrated on infancy, childhood, and adolescence. In recent years, however, there has been increasing interest in the physiological, psychological, and adaptive problems of maturity and old age.

Child psychologists have studied children's intellectual and emotional development, reasoning, moral concepts, the beginnings of social behavior in infancy, the development of language, the process of socialization (learning society's valued attitudes and behaviors), the origins of attitudes toward self and others, awareness of the self, the effects of day care, and many other aspects of development. Such knowledge is important because it provides an understanding of the origins of behavior and processes of growth and contributes to the planning of programs of child rearing, education, and recreation.

Students of the psychology of adolescence have been concerned with similar problems at a higher age level. Thus, at this age level they are concerned with developmental tasks of adolescence, such as advancing toward intellectual maturity, developing emotional independence of the home and family, making the transition from economic dependence on the home to being a self-sustaining and responsible individual in adult society, and approaching courtship and marriage.

Developmental psychologists concerned with adulthood have studied the adjustments typical of the prime of life, including the problems that confront people whose children have grown up and left home and those of men and women who, in mid-career, find themselves questioning their roles and their goals. Psychologists interested in old age have been concerned with the aging process, the effects of aging on self-concept, the effects of retirement, the relationship between pattern of life and work before retirement, the nature of the changes taking place in aptitudes and interests in old age, and other similar questions.

Many of the questions asked by developmental psychologists have implications for programs and policies in institutions such as hospitals and schools as well as more widely in the community. Those who are particularly interested in these issues have begun to conceptualize a new subdiscipline of applied developmental psychology to focus efforts toward a developmental perspective on challenges, such as minimizing the distress of hospitalized children, promoting healthy parent-child relations, and preventing teenage drug abuse and violence.

The developmental psychologist may conduct research in hospital newborn nurseries, day care centers, elementary or high schools, adult education centers, and homes for the aged. Playgrounds, scout meetings, a street corner meeting place, or a sandlot baseball field may also provide the locale for research. The developmental psychologist only rarely works in industry and is more often found at large in the community or in a specially equipped university laboratory.

The training of developmental psychologists includes the usual core studies in general, along with experimental and theoretical psychology. Some of these courses may be taken at the undergraduate level along with work in biology, sociology, and cultural anthropology. In addition, the developmental psychologist will take specialized courses in the psychology of childhood and adolescence and the psychological problems of adulthood and old age, supported by considerable work in personality, theoretical, educational, and social psychology. Observational methods, measurements, and fieldwork also play an important part in training. The doctorate degree is necessary for employment above the assistant or technician level.

Developmental psychologists are often employed in colleges and universities, particularly in departments of education and teachers colleges. Their principal function is teaching, although they may conduct research either as part of their work or on their own. Developmental psychologists also hold research positions in institutes devoted to child welfare, old age, or educational research. These institutes frequently are attached to universities, such as the universities of Iowa, Minnesota, Florida, and California. Developmental psychologists may work in research laboratories connected with hospitals or homes for the aged. There also have been openings in parent education work and in writing and editing.

The emphasis on understanding infant, child, and adolescent development has led to a demand for psychologists with this type of training. The study of infants at risk from particular problems has linked developmental psychology to pediatrics. Interest in the educational implications of the theories of Jean Piaget and more recent cognitive studies has made for a greater relationship between child, experimental, and educational psychology. There is renewed interest in adult development, joining developmental psychology with other specialties such as personality psychology and counseling, as well as academic insights with business and management. And finally, a growing elderly population has promoted greater interest in their functioning and needs.

Educational Psychology

The field of educational psychology is not easy to define. Although it is concerned with some problems that are most appropriately its own, it overlaps with certain other fields. A number of specialty fields, such as measurement, counseling, and school psychology, have largely broken away from educational psychology. What remains are teaching and research in the psychological problems of the educational process.

Human learning is one of the primary interests of the educational psychologist, as is the field of individual differences in abilities and interests. Both of these are obviously basic to education, as are: a) developmental psychology, because education is concerned with guiding and promoting development; b) social psychology, because children and adolescents are social creatures; and c) personality psychology, because education is concerned with the development of the whole person, with adjustment as well as with the acquisition of skills.

The educational psychologist draws on the knowledge and techniques of the school psychologist, the counseling psychologist, or the clinical psychologist. However, the distinguishing characteristic of the educational psychologist is a primary concern for psychological principles and techniques that have significance for educational problems. This professional is a student of educational problems, such as ability grouping and the education of the gifted, the handicapped, and the disadvantaged, with a primary interest in the implications of such problems as they relate to educational policies and processes.

It is clear that the educational psychologist must be a well-trained scientific and professional worker. Undergraduate work should be broad, stressing education and the social sciences. Good grounding in the basic fields of psychology—particularly learning theory—is essential, as is advanced work in developmental psychology, social psychology, personality theory, and measurement, including courses in which these fields are drawn together and applied to education.

Familiarity with the principles and techniques of counseling and guidance, some orientation toward clinical psychology, and competence in evaluation and measurement are also essential. It is desirable to have acquired some competence and experience as a practitioner in one of these fields and to be familiar with a variety of educational institutions and programs.

Research training and experimental design are especially important in this field. However, a crucial skill is the ability to understand classroom problems and communicate about them with teachers and administrators. This can come only with experience gained as a classroom teacher before, during, or after advanced study. Without this understanding, the psychologist's influence probably will not be significant.

Educational psychologists usually work in colleges and universities or in local, provincial, state, or federal boards of education. In colleges and universities, they are engaged in teaching educational psychology, measurement, individual differences, mental health, and related courses to prospective teachers and to teachers already in service. They also frequently supervise and conduct research with graduate students or a research institute.

In school systems, educational psychologists generally are employed in research bureaus. They may conduct routine operations in studying the abilities and achievements of pupils or, with increasing frequency, plan and carry out—cooperatively with curriculum and instruction specialists—studies in various methods of organizing and conducting classroom work.

The growth of developmental and counseling psychology, combined with the emphasis on mental health and clinical psychology, has led to more than one direction that educational psychologists can take. Some who stress theory have identified with developmental psychology or learning theory. Others with more applied interests become measurement specialists, mental health workers, or counseling psychologists. Still others direct their knowledge and skills toward the field of curriculum development and instruction.

Overall, the field of educational psychology can be seen as subdivided into two specialties. One is concerned with the development of learning abilities, an area that is basic to educational philosophy and methods. The other is primarily interested in new ideas and in the ways and means of getting these innovations into the mainstream of educational practice. Both instructors and research workers find challenging opportunities in these areas, not only at the doctoral level, but also at the M.A. level in positions as research assistants.

Psychology of Personality

The field of personality, either as a research area or as a focus of attention in educational and clinical practice, remains a popular and active field of psychology today. Many graduate students take courses and specialize in this field. In addition, many psychologists originally trained in other specialties have shifted their attention to this field and the kindred applied field of clinical psychology. With social psychology and psychometrics, the psychology of personality is the main area of scholarship and investigation basic to such service fields as clinical, counseling, and school psychology. There is much research going on in the psychology of personality, and many books are being published on this vital subject.

While psychologists historically have had some interest in the organic or physical bases of personality, their major concern in recent years has turned to its social aspects. They have studied the ways in which behavior is learned; the processes of conditioning and perception as they affect personality growth and functioning; the development of self-awareness and the enhancement and defense of the self; the influences on personality of various kinds of group memberships; the relationship between personality and culture; and the processes of personality integration and disintegration. Current projects in research and theory construction include the analysis of personality structure as a whole made up of interacting traits; the study of the need for selfhood as an integrative force in personality development; and investigation of the characteristic motives, perceptions, and actions by means of which a person interacts with others.

The work of the psychologist interested in personality may involve conducting research on certain narrowly defined problems, or it may concentrate on synthesizing the results of research in a variety of fields of psychology as they relate to theory of personality. Most theoretical treatises on the psychology of personality have been written by psychologists of the latter type or by theoretically inclined clinicians, in whose working lives research activities played a relatively small part. This separation of theory and research diminished somewhat during the years when research funds were made progressively more available to psychology as a field.

Personality theorists have studied the effects of infantile experience on the adult behavior of rats; the effects of social casework treatment on welfare families; the use of alcohol and marijuana and the effects of these drugs on attitudes and behavior; and the development of selfhood as shown in school children's essays on what they like and dislike about themselves. One group of psychologists explored the characteristics of the authoritarian personality. Others have concentrated on the statistical analysis of personality ratings in attempt to determine the basic dimensions of personality. Still others have tried to understand the limitations of a concept so broad as "personality"—that is, to look for the predictable inconsistencies in behavior as well as the consistencies that reflect personality.

Psychologists specializing in the field of personality should have in their undergraduate education considerable work in both the biological and social sciences, particularly the latter. Mathematics up to and through the study of calculus is important. A broad background in literature and history also helps give the perspective on people needed by a professional student of personality. Such preparation is more important than an extensive undergraduate background in psychology.

Graduate preparation should proceed to the doctorate level and include the basic courses in psychology. These courses should stress personality theory and developmental, social, and abnormal psychology with considerable work in measurement and research methods. Supplementary work in cultural anthropology and sociology is essential. Some experience and skill in clinical and counseling methods generally has been considered useful in personality research. A period of time spent in full-time research after the completion of the doctorate is a highly desirable and increasingly common way of developing the research habits and insights necessary to continuing productivity in this important field.

Personality psychologists and social psychologists together constitute a small percentage of all doctoral psychologists. Few personality psychologists have only a master's degree. The jobs held by personality psychologists are largely in universities, involving both teaching and research responsibilities. There also are a number of positions at all professional levels in government service, such as the United States Public Health Service and the Office of Naval Research.

Some private social service agencies have established long-term research projects in personality and related areas. These sometimes are financed by grants from public funds or from foundations.

This is an important and established field in psychology, though not a large one as a specialty. There is much new interest in it, and there is a great need for really creative research workers and theorists trained at the highest levels. The prospects are that it will become more important as improved theory and techniques make new insights possible.

Social Psychology

Social psychology has been defined as the study of the interaction of individuals, of how they function in society and respond at the group level. It is concerned with how individuals become socialized, how they utilize social patterns in the world about them, how they develop within themselves the social attitudes they find in family and neighborhood groups, how they participate in community life, and how they affect the personality patterns of those with whom they come in contact.

Social psychologists study such subjects as the social behavior of children, focusing on the development of different types of social interaction as children mature; the relationship of interpersonal relations in the home to interpersonal relations in school and club groups; personal and social factors related to the development of cooperative and competitive behavior; bargaining in conflict situations and international tensions; social attitudes such as bias, their origins, and their relationship to social behavior; voting habits and factors related to them; and the roles of individuals in groups, the personal and social situational factors related to these roles, and the effects of changing situations on roles.

Applied social psychology is concerned with the applications of the principles and techniques of the field to practical situations and problems. It embraces activities of such seemingly divergent nature as propaganda, housing, community organization, community attitudes and relations, advertising, market research, public opinion polling, morale, communication, and group dynamics. Although the applications are quite different, the principles and procedures underlying these activities actually overlap considerably. They all pertain to the study of groups and to the behavior of individuals in groups.

Applied social psychologists work on such problems as the study of national characteristics as a guide to psychological warfare and the maintenance of peace; the effectiveness of public relations and advertising; the analysis of consumer buying habits; public opinion; measuring changes in morale with changes in working conditions; ascertaining how a group learns to work as a team rather than as a collection of individuals; how members of a jury relate to each other as deliberations proceed; and devising and evaluating methods of leadership in group activities. The list of applications is long, varied, vital, and fascinating. This field is involved in business, industry, social agencies, schools, community situations, the armed forces, and in every kind of situation where groups of men and women are found.

The training for social psychologists is somewhat similar to that for personality psychologists but with less emphasis on abnormal psychology and on clinical and counseling principles and techniques. There is more emphasis on social interaction, the analysis of group behavior, social roles, perception, and communication processes. A period of postdoctoral experience as a full-time researcher, even when the ultimate objective is graduate-level teaching, is highly profitable and increasingly common. A person aiming at undergraduate teaching would find this experience not as important but helpful nonetheless.

Most positions in social psychology, like those in personality psychology, are in universities, research institutes connected with universities, nonprofit organizations, government agencies such as the Department of Agriculture and the Department of Defense, and public opinion and market research consulting firms. The distinction between science and profession often breaks down here, some jobs in the area being largely scientific or theoretical in nature, some largely applied, and some a combination.

This field of psychology has experienced rapid growth over the last few decades. Social trends, such as public concern with issues of race and discrimination, environmentalism, war and peace, and the lag of social understanding behind such technical developments as the Internet and the use of atomic energy have accented the need for research, knowledge, and application in the social sciences.

Social psychology has, therefore, come into its own. This trend can be expected to continue, and there will be a demand for able research workers, teachers, and consultants.

Psychometrics and Quantitative Methods

The field of psychological measurement is one that, perhaps more than any other, has established psychology's place in the public's mind. The term *IQ* has become a household word, and the most common association with the word *psychological* would probably be the word *test*.

Psychometrics is the science of measuring human intellectual, emotional, and social characteristics and behavior, although the term *sociometric* is more properly applied to measuring some aspects of social behavior. It is concerned with the identification of characteristics that can be measured and with the development of methods for measuring them. Its next concern is with the adaptation or development of statistical methods for the treatment of measurement data gathered, the refinement of measures, and the testing of their value as measures in relation to what they are supposed to measure.

The field overlaps with all of those that have been described so far because its concern is the development of theories and the provision of instruments that can be used by practitioners in these fields. There are metric psychologists who work in the fields of experimental, developmental, educational, personality and social, and abnormal psychology. The peculiar subject matter of psychometrics is measurement and statistical method, always with the objective of ultimate application to the content of some other field or fields, although at the particular moment the work is being done, it may be strictly theoretical.

Some confusion may arise from the fact that the term *psychometrist*, or *psychometrician*, is applied to technicians who use psychometric instruments and not to the psychologist who specializes in the science of psychometrics. The difference between the pursuit of the science and the application of the techniques is considerable.

Psychologists specializing in the science of measurement work on problems such as devising suitable tasks, questions, or other procedures for the evaluation of intellectual, personality, educational, or social characteristics; creating methods of combining these elements into scales or tests that differentiate between varying amounts of the characteristic in question; determining the consistency and independence of the measures obtained; and ascertaining their relationship to other characteristics and to subsequent behavior. Other quantitative psychologists devise and work with new methods for studying changes in psychological functioning over time and new programs for statistical analysis.

If the psychologists' work involves devising new types of procedures and instruments for the measurement of previously unidentifiable characteristics, they are engaged in the science of psychometrics. If, on the other hand, they are engaged in the construction of additional measures of characteristics already in existence, they belong more in the applied field. The two types of work are, of course, frequently combined. At the Educational Testing Service, for instance, some staff members work largely on the development of new types of measures or new ways of handling data, while others are concerned primarily with the production of new forms of existing tests.

Specialists in psychometrics, perhaps more than most other psychologists, may resemble the popular description of the Ph.D., one who "knows more and more about less and less," for their field is one of methodology rather than of content. However, as their methods are applied to a variety of substantive fields, those who work on applications find it essential to become very broad in interest and knowledge.

Good undergraduate grounding in mathematics is essential—at least through calculus—supplemented by work in the physical, biological, and social sciences. Graduate studies should include basic psychology, supplemented by work in developmental, personality, social, and educational psychology, with intensive study of individual differences. They should also include various types of tests, measurement principles and methods, statistics, and mathematical statistics. Knowledge of computer applications is essential.

The field of measurement and evaluation is the applied branch of the more purely scientific field of psychometrics. Measurement psychologists are specialists in psychometrics who are more concerned with the application of existing techniques than with the theory of measurement or with the development of new kinds of statistical methods.

Applied measurement is concerned with selecting, constructing, and applying tests or other measures to problems, such as determining the effectiveness of a training program; with constructing, applying, and evaluating tests and other devices such as interview procedures for the selection, evaluation, and upgrading of students or employees; and with developing tests for use in counseling and guidance. The work of measurement psychologists differs from that of specialists in psychometrics mainly in its emphasis on applications rather than on theory and on the use of tests and test items rather than on statistical methods of treating test data.

Not many psychologists consider this their specialty, even when devoting themselves to it full-time; most view themselves as educational, industrial, or other substantive types of psychologists. In one survey, about 1 percent of psychologists named this as their specialty; about half of these psychologists had a doctoral degree.

Metric psychologists are employed in a great variety of situations, wherever behavior has to be measured and measures have to be developed. They teach measurement courses and related subjects in colleges and universities, and they work in educational and psychological research institutes connected with universities or schools. They are found in medical and social welfare research organizations that need assistance in developing and applying measures of the effectiveness of their work or in studying trends involving their service populations. They are employed in federal, state, provincial, and local government agencies concerned with selecting personnel, evaluating training, or studying attitudes. They work in business and industry in the study of personnel selection, employee morale and training, or in market and public opinion research. They find employment wherever other types of psychological specialists are found.

Jobs held by measurement psychologists are generally in the same settings as those of psychometricians. They include teaching related courses in colleges and universities. Test development and publishing companies such as the Psychological Corporation and the Educational Testing Service, consulting firms, and research bureaus such as those of large school systems and universities often have measurement psychologists on their staffs to direct and carry out technical aspects of their work. There is no specialty certification by professional associations in this field.

As better methods of measuring characteristics are devised, more people want more things measured. While psychometrics was once confined largely to the laboratory or to the school or college, it now has an important place in business, industry, government, the armed forces, medicine, and social welfare. The theoretical and applied often merge in this field, as in social psychology. A growing number of psychologists develop computer programs to help interpret test results.

Today, widespread concern for the appropriateness of standardized tests for members of minority and special groups, combined with questioning of the use of certain kinds of personal data for personnel selection, inhibits work on testing in some organizations and encourages innovative work in others.

In addition to the pressures resulting from an increased awareness of minorities and of related measurement problems, the so-called "truth-in-testing" movement has resulted in new work for measurement specialists. This consists to some extent of making sure that tests and test items can be justified logically and empirically to official bodies and to the inquiring public. This increases the need to demonstrate the usefulness of tests; to reconcile data collection with disclosure regulations, thus making the ability to answer correctly universal and nonpredictive; and to require more time from test experts in keeping the public properly informed.

The well-trained psychological measurement technician with an M.A. degree finds some demand for his or her services, and the well-educated, versatile, and personally effective metric psychologist with the doctorate is in demand and will continue to be.

Industrial-Organizational Psychology

Industrial-organizational psychology is the study of people at work and how they relate to work. The objective of this specialty is to develop and apply procedures that will result in the better utilization of personnel, the better functioning of organizations, and the maximum well-being of the worker. In this applied field, the principles and techniques of developmental, educational, personality, social, and measurement psychology are brought to bear on the problems of people in work situations. Also of concern to these psychologists is the human factor in production methods.

The focus is on understanding the work situation, developing procedures, and applying principles and procedures necessary to the wise selection, effective placement, training, upgrading, and successful supervision, management, and organization of employees. Individual differences, motivation, morale, the organization of groups, the functioning of individuals in groups, and measurement are all factors.

For nearly three generations, industrial-organizational psychologists (formerly called personnel psychologists) have worked on the techniques used to select people for various types of jobs. They are concerned with the development of interview and rating procedures and with tests that examine intelligence, aptitudes, interests, personality, and proficiency; they also evaluate the effectiveness of these tests.

Some psychologists engaged in this work are measurement psychologists. However, industrial-organizational psychologists have demonstrated usefulness in employee selection and are involved in the development and evaluation of training methods for workers, as well as job analysis and evaluation. In addition, they conduct in-service training for employees, evaluate employees for promotion, ascertain the nature of effective supervision and leadership, study management communication methods, study the underlying factors that relate to good or poor employee morale, evaluate the effectiveness of methods and programs designed to improve morale, and finally, relate such factors to production.

To be effective in a business setting, the industrial-organizational psychologist must have a distinct combination of qualities. In addition to being interested in research and psychology as a science, this professional must be able to use psychological skills in practical situations. The industrial-organizational psychologist must also be able to communicate an understanding of a situation to people of widely varying backgrounds in order to win their confidence and thus establish effective working relationships with all levels in the organizational structure. These abilities require social and emotional maturity and a wide background of practical experience, particularly in the business world.

For these reasons, it is desirable for an industrial-organizational psychologist to have actual work experience in an industrial or business organization, which will provide firsthand knowledge of the way organizations function. But some industrial-organizational psychologists do go directly from undergraduate training to full-time doctoral programs; such programs should then include a supervised internship.

Industrial-organizational psychologists should have a broad undergraduate education that includes work in the social and biological sciences, education, and, preferably, a major in psychology. A background in business administration or engineering is helpful, but in such instances more supplementary graduate work is needed in the fields already mentioned. At the graduate level, students can obtain technical competence in some personnel functions with one year of specialized training leading to the M.A. degree. This training offers the basis for work as a human resources technician and stresses work in individual differences, the psychology of personality, statistics, testing, interviewing, and job analysis, with some study of labor economics and personnel administration.

More advanced educational preparation for work in industrial-organizational psychology, generally leading to a doctorate degree, involves studying the basic psychology courses. This is essential for anyone who wants to qualify as a psychologist and is not possible in the brief technicians' training program. Studies should also include both basic and advanced courses in developmental psychology, the psychology of personality, social psychology, educational psychology, measurement, and group development. Some supplementary study of the sociology of industry, labor economics, and human resources management also is essential. An internship or period of field work is highly desirable, because it orients the student to a work situation and makes the problems being studied more meaningful.

Jobs for industrial-organizational psychologists are found in business and industry, in colleges and universities, in government and the armed forces, and in consulting firms. Many psychology professors in this specialty do consulting work, either as a part of their university work or independently. Some have consulting firms of their own.

The demand for highly trained industrial-organizational psychologists remains high as businesses merge, technological advances change the nature of work and many jobs, and a growing global economy alters the face of business in many fields. Positions for M.A.s, though not numerous, have been sufficient to absorb most people qualified at this level. Many beginning jobs are filled by those with bachelor's degrees, but the competition for these jobs is great, and securing one depends less on training than on practical experience, contacts, and personal characteristics.

The American Board of Examiners in Psychology issues a diploma in industrial and organizational psychology to psychologists meeting its educational and experience requirements. These requirements include a doctorate, five years of appropriate experience, and passing written, oral, and practical examinations.

Counseling Psychology

Counseling psychology is the study of people as individuals, with the objective of helping them to develop as fully as possible by making the best use of their abilities, interests, and opportunities. It is concerned with the development of principles, methods, and techniques that will be helpful in this work and in their application to people who might benefit from help in self-fulfillment. As an applied field, counseling psychology draws heavily on the basic fields of developmental, educational, personality, social, and metric psychology. It has much in common with both clinical psychology and industrial-organizational psychology. It brings standard principles and techniques to bear on problems of understanding and helping individuals, and it supplements them with research on problems that are either peculiar to or highlighted in counseling.

Counseling psychologists interview high school and college students, employees, persons in need of vocational rehabilitation, and people in general who have problems concerning personal, social, educational, and vocational development and adjustment. In addition to the interview technique, they use tests and observational methods to collect additional information about their clients as individuals, in groups, and in the environments where they live and work. All of this is done to help clients develop more fully and make better adjustments. They carry on research in the development and improvement of appraisal methods and counseling techniques. They study resources that may be helpful to their clients in improving social or vocational adjustments, and they may supervise the work of other counseling psychologists who are less experienced or less highly trained.

The training of counseling psychologists has been studied by committees of the professional association concerned with education leading up to and through the doctorate. The counselor trained in psychology who specializes in vocational guidance should have at least two years of graduate training, although nonpsychologically trained school counselors now typically have one year of graduate preparation. However, earning a Ph.D. opens up a greater variety of higher level opportunities.

Undergraduate studies should be broad, with courses in the social and biological sciences, including psychology and education. Graduate training should include work in developmental, educational, personality, social, and measurement psychology. It should also include courses designed to bring the principles of these fields to bear on problems of personal, marital, social, and vocational development and counseling. There should be some study of sociology, economics, the type of institutional setting in which the counselor will work, and particularly educational and occupational information and other resources helpful in counseling, too. Graduate students should be well trained in the techniques of appraisal and counseling, with provision for some supervised experience in the use of these methods with clients. The American Board of Examiners in Psychology issues a diploma in counseling psychology to psychologists with appropriate doctoral training and five years of experience who pass special written, oral, and practical examinations.

Doctoral education provides a better grounding in basic psychology, more advanced work in relevant psychological theory and counseling techniques, and particular familiarity with and training in research that is essential to creative work in the field and to the progress of the profession. It covers a total of four years and includes a year of internship either on a full-time basis in the third year of graduate study or on a half-time basis during the last two years of graduate work.

Counseling psychologists and vocational counselors work in colleges and universities, usually in university counseling centers, often teaching as well as counseling. They are found in community guidance centers, in employment bureaus and such social agencies such as the YMCA and Jewish welfare agencies, in rehabilitation centers, in public and private hospitals, in the Veterans Administration, in the armed forces, and in a limited number of business and industrial organizations. A significant number are employed in consulting firms, sometimes to do counseling and sometimes to do executive evaluation work (the clinical study of persons in or being considered for key executive positions). An increasing number are in the full-time private practice of counseling psychology, partly because of the increasing recognition of the role that trained counselors can play in helping with situational problems relating to families, communities, and work and partly because the clinical competencies of those trained at the doctoral level lead to private practice in therapeutic counseling. When demand and interest result in such work, the distinction between counseling and clinical psychologists becomes difficult to make, despite counseling's emphasis on developmental and educational work as contrasted with remedial or reconstructive work.

The demand for the services of counseling psychologists has soared toward the end of each war from World War II onward and is currently rising during the war in Iraq. Counseling services are needed by returning troops, displaced war-industry workers, and wounded and emotionally disturbed veterans. Former veterans' guidance centers generally were converted into permanent college or community counseling services, employing well-prepared counseling psychologists and vocational counselors. It was found in many situations that a staff composed of men and women trained at both the M.A. and Ph.D. or Ed.D. levels worked very effectively, setting a pattern now widespread in community colleges, four-year arts and engineering colleges, and universities.

Colleges and universities have employed counseling psychologists in other aspects of student personnel work, such as testing programs, discipline, mental health, student activities, and the direction of student services. Public school systems increasingly are seeking counseling psychologists with high school teaching experience as directors of guidance, and community guidance centers steadily have raised their standards and increased in number.

Counseling psychologists have taken on new roles in evaluating the employability of adults for the Social Security Administration and for vocational rehabilitation. The extension of insurance coverage, both governmental and private, to cover psychotherapy and, in some instances, vocational counseling designed to restore or to improve employability, also has opened new opportunities for counseling psychologists.

The Veterans Administration and the Rehabilitation Services Administration followed and assisted in these developments by raising standards, by supporting training programs in cooperation with a number of universities, and by employing a large number of well-trained counseling psychologists. Despite budget cuts, counseling psychology continues to offer opportunities in the services and programs of colleges, schools, community agencies, hospitals, and industries staffed by both M.A.s and Ph.D.s.

Clinical and Abnormal Psychology

Clinical psychology is the study and treatment of emotionally disturbed or intellectually deficient individuals. The disturbance may be slight, as in normal development, or serious, as in psychosis. The deficiency may also be minor, as in some learning disabilities, or serious, as in severe mental retardation. These people are studied to determine their actual and potential levels of functioning (in terms of both accomplishment and happiness) and to help them make adjustments appropriate to their capacities and opportunities.

Clinical psychology is the field of psychology most concerned with the development of principles, methods, and techniques to be applied to disturbed and handicapped people. In making these applications, it draws heavily on the basic fields of abnormal, developmental, personality, social, and metric psychology together with neurology, physiology, genetics, and sociology. It synthesizes them in the study of emotional disturbance and mental deficiency and adds to the relevant store of knowledge and tools by conducting its own research on its own particular problems.

Abnormal psychology is the study of mental and emotional disorders. It is concerned with the development, manifestations, and treatment methods of personality deviations and intellectual defects, both organic and functional. It is an important part of the scientific basis of clinical psychology and psychiatry and contributes to the understanding of the normal personality.

Psychologists working in this field may study the relationships between the structure and nature of family relationships and the incidence of schizophrenia; specific language dysfunctions caused by different loci of brain injury; and the differences in the responses of various types of disturbed individuals to psychological tests. These are also the research activities of clinical psychologists; most persons conducting research in or devoting most of their time to teaching abnormal psychology are clinical psychologists. There are a few exceptions, particularly experimental or physiological psychologists or students of personality, who have directed their research activities into this area and who make a special contribution through the use of the most highly developed concepts and methods in their fields.

A clinical psychologist interviews a patient to get an understanding of the patient's background and status, or the psychologist may rely on case reports if the patient is too disturbed, young, or deficient to be interviewed. Clinical psychologists may interview relatives or associates to see the patient as others do. They administer tests to obtain a more objective and well-rounded picture of the patient and write diagnostic reports concerning the patient. They may discuss the patient with psychiatrists, social workers, pediatricians, judges, and other specialists who refer cases for diagnostic study or with whom they work in a team relationship, as well as with parents, teachers, or physicians. Clinical psychologists may counsel the patient, provide psychotherapy, or refer the patient to another type of service. They may supervise other psychologists with less experience and training. Their activities may also include conducting research in psychodiagnosis and psychotherapy and teaching related courses.

Undergraduate studies include courses in psychology, biological and physical sciences, mathematics and statistics, education, social sciences, history of culture, psychology as revealed in literature, and languages. The goal is a broad liberal education with work in certain areas necessary for graduate work in psychology.

In graduate training, the objective in most universities is to produce a psychologist who is acquainted with the basic areas of psychological theory, research, and methods. This should include such subjects as general psychology (physiological and comparative, history and schools of psychology, developmental psychology and psychopathology), diagnostic methods, therapy, research methods, and related disciplines (physiology, related medical information, social organization and social pathology, and cultural anthropology). In a few programs, there is less emphasis on general psychology and research, with the objective of preparing practitioners. The program may take four years and includes a full-time internship during the third year or a half-time internship during the third and fourth years.

There has been much discussion of the need for standards in the training of clinical technicians below the doctoral level. Some colleges and universities offer an M.A. in clinical psychology. Unlike the field of counseling psychology, however, clinical psychology has as yet reached no agreement to standardize such programs, much less their content. The American Board of Examiners in Psychology issues a diploma in clinical psychology to highly qualified clinicians comparable to those given in industrial and counseling psychology.

Another important trend in the development of clinical psychology—arising from interest in practicing rather than in doing research and a sometimes associated belief that research training is irrelevant to or interferes with training in psychodiagnostics and psychotherapy—has been the development of schools of professional psychology. Such schools are more clinical and generally disregard counseling—industrial, organizational, engineering, and school psychology. They offer a practitioner's degree, usually the Psy.D. The admission requirement is an undergraduate degree with an emphasis on psychology, but these schools are generally less influenced by traditional standards than are the graduate schools of the stronger universities.

As a result of the emphasis on doctoral education and the uncertain status of subdoctoral training in clinical psychology, the best positions in this field are generally open only to those who have Ph.D.s. Clinical psychologists with the Ph.D., Psy.D., or Ed.D. are employed in universities accredited for graduate training in this field and in other colleges and universities as instructors in this specialty. They also work in university clinics, medical schools, and hospitals as clinicians and research workers. They are employed in the Veterans Administration, the United States Public Health Service, and the armed forces.

Many also work in institutions for the delinquent or mentally defective, in prisons, in public and private hospitals, in mental health or child guidance clinics, and in psychological clinics sponsored by community organizations. Others are employed in consulting firms doing executive evaluation (clinical personnel) work. Finally, there are many in private practice, some of whom work in cooperation with other practitioners, such as psychiatrists, pediatricians, and social workers; others work independently. Clinical psychologists without the doctorate are most generally employed in junior staff positions or in institutions that are unable to compete for fully qualified clinicians.

As already mentioned, the demand for clinical psychologists increased beyond all precedent or expectation toward the end of World War II and surged again after other major military efforts. This increase is partly because of the number of emotionally inadequate or disturbed members of the service who need help and partly because of an increased public awareness of the importance of human resources and human adjustment. To meet this need, large-scale programs were set up by the Veterans Administration and the United States Public Health Service after World War II and a smaller program by the army for the training of clinical psychologists at the doctoral level. Furthermore, the American Psychological Association assumed the responsibility of evaluating and accrediting graduate training in clinical psychology, a move that has since been expanded to include concern for psychological training in all applied areas. Actual accrediting is done only when requested by outside fund-granting agencies for such fields as clinical, counseling, and school psychology, and upon request by the university.

School Psychology

School psychologists often have functioned as clinical psychologists in an educational setting. They are concerned with problems of adjustment, mental health, and school achievement, primarily in elementary schools. School psychology has therefore drawn on the basic fields of developmental, personality, social, and metric psychology together with physiology, sociology, social work, educational psychology, and educational philosophy. It makes its own synthesis of these other fields to understand children who have problems adjusting to school. It endeavors to help them directly as well as through their parents and teachers to make better adjustments and get the most from their educational opportunities. In the process, school psychologists conduct research to make better applications of their techniques and to provide themselves with more effective working tools.

More than ever before, school psychologists have a broad responsibility for the educational adjustment and mental health of students. They work with teachers, administrators, and parents to develop healthy emotional and effective learning experiences for children. School psychologists may work with a group of teachers on a problem such as the psychological factors involved in the poor scholastic achievement of bright children. They also may participate as members of teams in clarifying procedures related to the classification of pupils, the development of a desirable program for induction of children into kindergarten, a survey of progress in particular fields of academic achievement, or the evaluation of a new program. Intensive study is made into any troublesome area involving a student's personal development when requested by the principal, teacher, or supervisor.

School psychologists also administer group and individual tests to children to ascertain their intellectual and proficiency levels and to locate areas in which they need additional assistance. They interview children and conduct play therapy with them for diagnostic purposes. School psychologists also interview parents and teachers to round out their pictures of the children. They observe the children in work and play situations. They write up diagnostic reports and case studies in special instances and then discuss these with other specialists at child guidance clinics, health centers, or in school staff conferences.

School psychologists generally refer those children who require psychotherapy to other agencies, although in some instances they may conduct it themselves. In addition, they may do some parent counseling. Increasingly, school psychologists work through classroom teachers to bring about better adjusted children. They may also supervise remedial teaching or special classroom work for slow learners or handicapped children. More and more, they act as staff consultants and contribute to the study and solution of curricular and instructional problems that involve psychological understanding or techniques.

The principal emphasis in the education of school psychologists is on working effectively with teachers and helping them improve their handling of children's problems. Increasingly, school psychologists are expected to assume leadership in helping teachers, administrators, and curriculum workers develop programs in accordance with sound learning and developmental principles and to be a force in helping the community understand and accept needed school changes.

Until recently, the education of most school psychologists ended with the master's degree. As in other specialties, however, the need for higher standards has become evident, and an increasing number of school psychologists are earning doctoral degrees. The importance of more advanced education is evident, as today's school psychologist plays a more important role in education as a diagnostician, therapist, supervisor of child development and remedial education, curriculum consultant, and participant in the program of in-service education for teachers.

The American Psychological Association's Education and Training Board and its Division of School Psychologists have studied educational standards in this field. They recommended two preparatory programs for school psychologists. The first is a two-year training program, open only to teachers who have taught in elementary or secondary schools. The other is a three-year doctoral program. On the undergraduate level, work in education is preferred. On the graduate level, the work should stress developmental, educational, personality, social, and measurement psychology with supporting work in physiology, sociology, and education. In addition, there should be intensive work in the diagnostic and therapeutic techniques involved in this area of psychology, which should be supplemented by supervised practice in individual work with children in schools and clinics and in consulting with teachers and school administrators. The advantage of doctoral work is that it permits the inclusion of more work in diagnostic and treatment techniques, personality theory, research, and practical experience.

While most school psychologists have a doctorate, a larger number of school psychologists have training only at the master's level. Like educational psychology, school psychology has traditionally attracted many women; unlike it, school psychology employs many M.A.s. This may become less true as consulting and program evaluation roles expand.

School psychologists work in public and private schools and occasionally in school psychological clinics. Usually, however, especially in public schools, they work for the board of education, making visits to individual schools. Those with doctoral training frequently transfer to teaching positions in colleges and universities.

Those who remain with a board of education may advance to director of guidance or supervisor of psychological services for a school system. This is particularly true of those school psychologists whose education and experience have given them training in counseling psychology and those who have worked with adolescents. School psychologists who have had extensive experience with exceptional children often will advance to administrative positions in special education programs.

School psychologists must be certified by their state or province to work in a public school system. The requirements for certification vary by locality, but they can usually be met in one year of properly planned graduate work. Students should check the requirements of the areas in which they expect to be employed and plan a program of study with these requirements in mind.

The demand for well-trained and effective school psychologists is considerable. The development of special programs for disadvantaged and special-needs children highlights this need.

Sports Psychology

Sports psychologists are concerned with the psychological stimuli that affect and improve athletic performance. They also look at the effects of exercise and physical activity on psychological adjustment and health. Sports psychologists typically work in academic settings and/or as consultants for sports teams. They often work in conjunction with sports medicine professionals.

Emerging Specialties, Related Fields, and Interdisciplinary Bridges

As the specialties of psychology mature and branch out to meet new challenges, several new fields of interest have developed, in effect becoming emerging specialties. Most of these involve building bridges to other disciplines, usually around applied issues. One of the more prominent is health psychology, a field that combines aspects of physiological, social, counseling, and clinical psychology. Whether practitioners or researchers, health psychologists study the role of psychological functioning in the promotion of health and the prevention and treatment of illness. Thus, their research or applied work may focus on the origins or treatments of obesity, smoking, and cardiovascular disease, or on the management of stress and adherence to a prescribed program of medication and exercise. A growing number of universities offer doctoral programs in health psychology, which continues to advance due to scientific progress and available research funds.

A related field is pediatric psychology, where clinical and developmental psychologists conduct research on aspects of medical practice that are unique to children. This may include such issues as how to help a child with leukemia adapt to the difficult medical regimen and the massive disruption of daily life or the optimal policy on a parent staying overnight in a hospital with a young patient. Pediatric psychologists who actively work with patients are initially trained as clinicians, and they have taken additional practical or internship training to specialize.

Another emerging specialty is family psychology, which is concerned with the understanding and improvement of family dynamics and individual development within the family. Again, both research and applied issues dominate discussion in this field, and family psychologists might be primarily researchers or clinicians trained in family therapy.

Forensic psychology is a rapidly growing area of specialization. It is concerned with the theoretical and applied study of psychology and the law in such areas as investigating the mental competence of a person to stand trial, assessing neuropsychological damage of accident victims, and evaluating the relative strengths and weaknesses of two divorcing parents who each want custody of a child. Specialization in psychology and the law is usually achieved within another, more traditional program (such as clinical or social psychology), often with postdoctoral training.

Cross-cultural psychology is also gaining momentum. Some of the impetus for this comes from a theoretical appreciation of culture as an organizing context for the development and regulation of behavior, and some comes from the increasing international communication of psychologists around the world. What was once a near monopoly by American scientists has become global in its application and activity, and cross-cultural psychology attempts to understand the diversity of results around the world and use this perspective to improve our theories of human behavior.

A small number of universities offer advanced degrees in cross-cultural psychology. The specialty may also be achieved within a more traditional field, such as social or developmental psychology.

In all of these areas, psychologists find themselves working with and drawing on the literature of colleagues in anthropology, law, medicine, biology, and other related fields. Innovations in these fields are often exciting and productive, and some are attracting significant research funds. They are some of the most rapidly growing areas and among the most appealing to students.

3

EDUCATION AND TRAINING

As YOU HAVE seen in the last chapter, psychology is a demanding field that requires much preparation for its practitioners. Regardless of the area of specialization, psychologists are charged with tremendous responsibility in treating patients and making recommendations, and the level of preparation required exceeds the limits of an undergraduate degree.

In its early days, psychology was a profession dominated by college teachers, who have always needed advanced degrees. As increasing numbers of psychologists began to work in settings other than colleges, the need for graduate preparation was reinforced by the need for a broad understanding combined with mastery of a substantial body of technical knowledge. Psychologists employed in medical settings found that if their special skills and instruments were to be used effectively, they had to be professional workers with the depth and breadth of understanding of psychology, behavior, and physiology that enabled them to work with physicians as their peers.

Psychologists working in schools and colleges in nonteaching capacities must be students of people and of society with a broad understanding of educational problems and processes. Psychologists engaged in the application of psychology to business and industry must be scientific and professional workers with considerable training if they are to have success in putting psychology to work.

Undergraduate Education

For these reasons, undergraduate education in psychology is considered nonprofessional in nature. The position of the American Psychological Association, as expressed by various committees, conferences, and its Education and Training Board, is that the undergraduate study of psychology has general educational value that gives it an important place in college curricula but that it cannot and should not attempt to prepare people for work as psychologists, except in laying a foundation for a higher degree.

Your undergraduate study leading to career preparation as a psychologist should include a substantial amount of work in psychology (not necessarily as a major). The program of study should be designed to give you a fair acquaintance with the content of the field, both in its general and in its laboratory aspects. Courses in general, experimental, physiological, developmental, personality, social, educational, and metric psychology are desirable, along with some work in the history of psychology.

You should include courses in the natural sciences, particularly in biology (including genetics). Some work in chemistry and physics also should be included, based on your ultimate objectives and the amount of physical science you studied in high school. You will also need college work in mathematics and statistics, with an emphasis on principles.

The social sciences should also be an important part of your undergraduate program. If you already have a clear idea about your future area of specialization, you will emphasize either natural science or social science. For example, an aspiring clinical psychologist may emphasize the biological sciences, a future counseling psychologist may stress the social sciences, and a potential experimental psychologist may give equal emphasis to physiology and physics. Regardless of the specialty you choose, however, you should be well grounded in each of these fields. In the social sciences, sociology and anthropology seem most important, but economics, political science, and history also are relevant.

Humanities courses such as literature, art, philosophy, and religion are also important components of a degree program, as they offer insights into the needs and desires of society. Good writing and speaking skills are of vital importance. A psychologist—whether planning to be a teacher, research worker, clinician, or personnel administrator—must know how to organize and present facts and ideas in ways that are readily understood by and interesting to a variety of audiences.

An undergraduate program should include experiences that help you to develop into an effective and interesting person. These experiences will vary widely because of differences in personality, interests, and abilities, but they should include activities that enable you to develop and use social skills in small groups, larger groups, and interpersonal relations.

Graduate Preparation

Becoming a psychologist involves getting over a number of hurdles. The first of these is getting into college, and the second is graduating from college. Next comes getting into a graduate school, then obtaining a master's degree (a step skipped by many who move directly from completing the B.A. to studying for the doctorate). This is followed by acceptance as a doctoral candidate, successfully completing all required courses, passing a comprehensive examination, completing a doctoral dissertation or research project, and finally, in most universities, defending the doctoral dissertation in an oral examination. The number of people overcoming each hurdle becomes fewer as the hurdles get higher.

Universities generally try to weed out the intellectually and emotionally unqualified as early as possible. They attempt to select only those students who are considered likely to complete their studies. Moreover, the better universities seek to admit only as many students as can be handled effectively and, on completion of their studies, can be placed in appropriate jobs. Within these objectives, however, methods vary considerably, and it is beneficial for the prospective student to know how the institution he or she is considering operates.

Your selection for admission to a master's and doctoral program will be based partly on your intellectual ability as shown by college grades, achievement examinations, and scholastic aptitude tests. The Graduate Record Examination (achievement and aptitude) and the Miller Analogies Test (aptitude) were devised especially for these purposes. Ratings by college teachers also are used in an attempt to assess intellectual characteristics such as originality, resourcefulness, judgment, industriousness, motivation, and scholarliness.

As a candidate for training in most of the applied or professional fields, you will also be evaluated on your interest in people as individuals rather than as subjects for study. In addition, your sensitivity to social situations, warmth, tact, insight, emotional stability, and ethical standards will also be evaluated.

If you are considering teaching psychology, you are likely to be judged by your obvious desire to share knowledge with others, your skill in doing so, and your interest in keeping up with new developments in the field.

In preparing for primarily scientific positions, you will be judged by your interest in theory as well as your concern for facts and your skill and creativity in defining problems, in designing research, and in applying scientific methods to solutions.

Evidence of these characteristics generally is gathered during the course of graduate study as well as during undergraduate work. The first year often is designed partly to provide appropriate opportunities for judging. Undergraduate teachers also often know students well enough to make judgments concerning promise and performance in these areas and are skillful in setting up situations in which students can demonstrate these characteristics.

Master's Programs

The master of arts (or science or education) degree requires one or two years of graduate study, depending on the institution or department. Most institutions believe that only average or better-than-average college students should be admitted to work for the M.A. degree. Some institutions, however, admit any college graduate, and a few admit only potential doctoral candidates.

In the first two types of graduate schools, the master's program may be perceived as a proving ground for doctoral candidates in which students have a chance to show what they can do. It may be planned as a terminal program, designed to prepare students for work in some specialty. Or it may attempt to do both things at once. Many institutions that offer the master's degree do not offer the doctorate. In this case, the student who wants to continue must apply to another institution and transfer on completion of the degree.

With such variations in M.A. programs, it is important to know the program and policy of the institution you are considering. First, does admission mean that you have been carefully screened and are considered a good doctoral candidate? Does it mean that your records have been evaluated and that you are considered a good candidate for the M.A., with the idea that time will tell about the doctorate? Or does it merely mean that you are being allowed to find out whether or not you are really master's caliber?

In addition, will the program offer the necessary preparation for employment, or will a Ph.D. also be necessary? If the former is true, is the specialty one in which you will be satisfied and in which employment prospects for M.A.s are good? As we have seen in Chapter 2, there are differences among fields: a master's degree in counseling, school psychology, or measurement, for example, is more marketable than one in experimental or social psychology. If the latter is the case (and this is true of some excellent programs), what percentage of students completing the M.A. are able to continue toward the doctorate? Which type of program will be best for you?

Doctoral Programs

The degree doctor of philosophy (or psychology or education) generally requires three or four years of graduate study, including the M.A., and often takes five years because of the time required for completing a research project. As already pointed out, completion of the M.A. is by no means a guarantee of admission to a doctoral program. In fact, admission to a doctoral program probably is the most difficult hurdle of all to surmount, and more would-be students are eliminated at that point than at any other.

While some institutions consider it wise to use the master's program as a proving ground for doctoral work, most of the better universities prefer to admit as doctoral candidates only those they think are likely to complete their program of studies and to have them begin their graduate work as doctoral students. Transferring from an M.A. program to a Ph.D. program is difficult, if not impossible, in such institutions. Even then, the comprehensive examination still screens out some, and a few others fail to complete a dissertation.

If you are unsure of pursuing a doctoral degree but apply to a doctorate-granting institution for admission as a master's candidate, you will have the opportunity to demonstrate your abilities early in the course of graduate work. This will enable you to make more confident decisions concerning doctoral candidacy and may be better than applying with an M.A. from another institution. On the other hand, if you want a doctorate and are admitted directly to the program of a selective institution, you will have the greater advantage of earning your degree and moving directly toward your career goal.

Doctoral programs, like master's programs, vary from one university to another. Some departments of psychology, for example, have long emphasized experimental psychology. In the past, some administrations have contended that this should be the training of all psychologists, no matter what the later specialization will be. Other universities have emphasized the preparation of students equipped for intensive work in some of the special fields of psychology and thus have APA-approved programs in most of the applied fields.

These variations really are not as great as such a statement may make them seem. It is generally recognized that a psychologist should, first of all, be a psychologist and that specialization should represent expert ability in—rather than limitation to—a special field. So the type of doctoral program approved by the Education and Training Board of the American Psychological Association today is one in which all doctoral candidates in psychology are well grounded in the basic courses and in which specialists in such fields as clinical, counseling, and school psychology are offered appropriate opportunities for the more advanced and intensive study of their specialties.

Postdoctoral Programs

For many years, postdoctoral preparation in psychology existed in informal and unsystematic ways, but today's programs are formalized and more common in most specialties. For example, college psychology teachers who wanted to shift to research or applied positions occasionally took such positions at nominal salaries and with supervision, allowing them to master the special skills and acquire the special knowledge of the new field. Today, postdoctoral training in clinical psychology is provided at centers such as the Postgraduate Center for Mental Health in New York and the Menninger Foundation in Topeka, Kansas; in shorter courses given at some universities; and in connection with the annual meeting of the American Psychological Association.

Postdoctoral training in research is offered by a number of research institutes, many of them located at universities. The Social Science Research Council and the National Research Council offer fellowships for postdoctoral research training. The Ford Foundation and the National Science Foundation also contributed to developments of this type.

At all levels, students in the applied fields need opportunities to apply their knowledge and use their skills under expert supervision. This supervised experience is known as *practicum training* and generally is required in clinical, counseling, industrial-organizational, school, and applied social psychology. Such experience is also necessary in many of the theoretical fields, for example, in the laboratory work of the experimental psychologist, the nursery school and elementary school observation of the developmental psychologist, the field studies of the social psychologist, and the apprentice teaching of the graduate student with a teaching assistantship.

Before deciding on a university for graduate education, find out what types of practicum training (including research) are available. In clinical psychology, for example, practicum training normally is preceded by laboratory training at the university in the use of psychological tests, interviewing, and observational techniques. It includes clerkship-level training in the application of these techniques to patients or clients who are being studied by fully qualified psychologists.

The next level of practicum training is internship experience in which the student studies and works with patients in a way that, by the end of the internship, approximates that of a junior staff member. In all of these activities, the work should be supervised; that is, the early testing should be observed and the test protocols corrected; later diagnostic reports should be reviewed and edited; psychotherapeutic work should be discussed (this last takes one-half hour or more of supervisory time for each hour spent with a patient); and relationships with clients and professional colleagues should be observed and reviewed.

Continuing Education

Like professionals in other areas, psychologists are increasingly interested in brief, intensive courses or workshops that are classified as continuing education. These programs may consist of a weekend seminar on new statistical techniques or an afternoon session on the psychologist's role in legal issues of criminal insanity. Many psychologists find continuing education workshops an efficient way to keep up with recent developments and acquire new skills. Also, a certain number of hours at certified sessions is required by many states for keeping a valid license to practice psychology.

Accredited Graduate Programs in Psychology

One way to find out which institutions offer good programs of education for a science or profession is to get a list of those that have been accredited by the appropriate scientific or professional association—in this case the American Psychological Association (APA). The APA has an Education and Training Board that coordinates the work of a number of committees dealing with special aspects of psychological training.

The APA accredits doctoral programs in clinical, counseling, and school psychology; some other developed practice areas; and any combination of two or three of these areas. Predoctoral internships in any of these areas may also be accredited, as well as postdoctoral residencies in traditional or specialty areas. The Canadian Psychological Association (CPA) handles accreditation of these programs in Canada. Complete information on accreditation is available from the APA at www.apa.org/ed/accreditation, and from the CPA at www.cpa.ca/accreditation.

Choosing a Graduate School

Given all of this information, how should you choose a university for graduate work in psychology? There are a number of steps to follow, all of which will provide helpful information along the way. The APA- and CPA-approved lists can be used as guides for work in clinical, counseling, and school psychology and as indications that the institutions approved for work in these fields also have adequate supporting work in the basic fields. Remember that some of the best work in fields other than the three evaluated fields is offered by universities that do not have applied psychology programs.

Check the general reputation of the university as a graduate school, based on information from your college faculty members and from psychologists with whom you have contact.

The directories of the American Psychological Association, the American Psychological Society, and the Canadian Psychological Association are also helpful. They provide geographical directories that group psychologists by institutions, making it possible to look up individual psychologists in different parts of the country in order to ascertain their training and experience levels.

Also useful are the journal *American Psychologist* and the APA *Monitor*, which can provide information about what is happening at various universities, who is conducting research projects, and where research grants are being funded. Presumably, foundations and the government give money and contracts to universities they have evaluated and found appropriate for their purposes.

The *Psychological Bulletin*, the *Annual Review of Psychology*, *Contemporary Psychology*, *Psychology Today*, and other psychology magazines and journals publish reviews of research, book reviews, and other articles that offer insight into what kind of work is being done by university staff members and how it is being received by other psychologists.

The approved lists of the APA are published each year in the *American Psychologist*; these data usually are included in the November issue. *Graduate Study in Psychology* publishes related data, such as the numbers of each kind of degree granted, the fields in which work is offered, admission procedures, and fellowships and stipends.

Financing Graduate Education

It may seem daunting to think about funding one to five years of graduate education. With rising tuition rates, plus the cost of room, meals, laundry, clothing, transportation, books, and supplies, one year of study can easily require more than $30,000, possibly much more depending on the institution. One way of cutting costs is to obtain a full-time job at or near the university and attend classes on a part-time basis. Unfortunately, this will extend the length of your studies and impact the amount of time you can devote to concentrating on classes.

Fellowships, loans, and assistantships generally are the answer. Institutions offering graduate work usually have a number of scholarships, fellowships, teaching assistantships, and research assistantships open to graduate students, as well as loan funds available without collateral. Some departments admit only students whom they can, in effect, support.

Scholarships and fellowships must be applied for in advance. They are awarded on a competitive basis, merit being judged by grades, examinations, and recommendations. They range from small scholarships granting exemption from tuition to more generous fellowships that provide full—if modest—support. These last fellowships are, of course, relatively scarce and much sought after.

Information concerning such awards is given in university catalogs and is announced along with assistantships each year in *Graduate Study in Psychology*, published by the APA. The university to which one is applying may be a very helpful source of information.

The United States Public Health Service provides fellowships in clinical, child, physiological, and social psychology with stipends that vary with the level of training, plus tuition and fees. The Veterans Administration appoints students of clinical and counseling psychology to training positions in which they give about half of their time to a VA internship and the other half to graduate study at stipends that also depend on training and experience; this does not include tuition. The Rehabilitation Services Administration provides traineeships for master's as well as for doctoral candidates at similar levels, with extras for tuition, fees, and dependents. These appointments are made by the university departments after the student has been admitted as a doctoral candidate. National Science Foundation (NSF) fellowships for the basic fields in psychology also provide stipends plus tuition, fees, and dependents' allowances. Application for these fellowships is made directly to the NSF.

Teaching assistantships usually are open only to students already in residence at a university and often are for small sums only. They may involve grading papers for a course with a stipend of a few hundred dollars for the semester. On the other hand, they may involve teaching sections of a large course at a stipend of several thousand dollars, sometimes with tuition exemption. In the long run, the experience often is as important as the stipend. It brings the student into more intimate contact with faculty members and introduces the student to the teaching profession.

Research assistantships sometimes are open to new students, but more often they are available only to those already in residence at a university. The duties involve working with faculty members and other research staff on research projects. These projects may be financed by grants from foundations, by institutional funds, or by industrial or government contracts. This type of financial assistance, like teaching assistantships, can have considerable educational value.

It is important to research scholarships, fellowships, and teaching and research assistantships ahead of time. Part-time jobs and student loans are other possibilities. In some cases, students work full-time for two or three years after college to save money for graduate school. Whichever road you choose, be sure to consider all the options. If you plan to borrow money, understand all the terms of repayment and be prepared to meet those demands when the time comes. If you are awarded an assistantship, you must be prepared to do the extra work that will be required to earn your stipend.

4

Employment Prospects and Compensation

Employment of psychologists is expected to grow faster than the average for all occupations over the next decade. In fact, employment is expected to grow as much as 15 percent through 2016 because of increased demand for psychological services in schools, hospitals, social service agencies, mental health centers, substance abuse treatment clinics, consulting firms, and private companies.

Employment growth will vary by specialty. For example, growing awareness of how students' mental health and behavioral problems such as bullying affect learning will increase demand for school psychologists to offer student counseling and mental health services.

Prevention and treatment have become more critical issues in light of the rise in health care costs associated with unhealthy lifestyle choices such as smoking, alcoholism, and obesity.

An increase in the number of employee assistance programs that help workers deal with personal problems also should lead to employment growth for clinical and counseling specialties. Clinical and counseling psychologists will be needed to help people deal with depression and other mental disorders, marriage and family problems, job stress, and addiction.

The growing number of elderly will increase the demand for psychologists trained in geropsychology. They will be needed to help people deal with the mental and physical changes that occur as individuals grow older. There also will be increased need for psychologists to work with returning veterans.

Industrial-organizational psychologists will be in demand to help boost worker productivity and retention rates in a wide range of businesses. They will help companies deal with issues such as workplace diversity and antidiscrimination policies. Companies also will use psychologists' expertise in survey design, analysis, and research to develop tools for marketing evaluation and statistical analysis.

Master's Degree Holders

Graduates with a master's degree in psychology may find work as industrial-organizational psychologists. They also may work as psychological assistants under the supervision of doctoral-level psychologists and may conduct research or psychological evaluations.

Those who have master's degrees in fields other than industrial-organizational psychology will face keen competition for jobs because of the limited number of positions that require only a master's degree. Master's degree holders may find jobs as psychological assistants or counselors, providing mental health services under the direct supervision of a licensed psychologist. Still others may find jobs involving research and data collection and analysis in universities, government, or private companies.

A master's degree in psychology requires at least two years of full-time graduate study. Requirements usually include practical experience in an applied setting and a master's thesis based on an original research project. Competition for admission to graduate psychology programs is keen. Some universities require applicants to have an undergraduate major in psychology; others prefer only coursework in basic psychology with additional courses in the biological, physical, and social sciences and in statistics and mathematics.

Bachelor's Degree Holders

As is expected, opportunities directly related to psychology will be limited for bachelor's degree holders. Some may find jobs as assistants in rehabilitation centers or in other jobs involving data collection and analysis. Those who meet state certification requirements may become high school psychology teachers.

A bachelor's degree in psychology qualifies a person to assist psychologists and other professionals in community mental health centers, vocational rehabilitation offices, and correctional programs. Bachelor's degree holders may also work as research or administrative assistants for psychologists. Some work as technicians in related fields, such as marketing research. Many find employment in other areas, such as sales, service, or business management.

In the federal government, candidates having at least twenty-four semester hours in psychology and one course in statistics qualify for entry-level positions. However, competition for these jobs is keen because this is one of the few ways in which to work as a psychologist without an advanced degree.

Rapid Growth

The majority of psychologists in North America belong to the American Psychological Association (APA) or the Canadian Psychological Association (CPA). The organizations have 148,000 members and 6,000 members, respectively; growth of each has increased steadily since their inception, particularly in the last twenty years. There is no indication that this growth will abate, as psychology continues to be one of the most popular undergraduate and graduate fields of study.

The mere increase in the number of psychologists is important but not sufficient for someone considering the opportunities in the field. Where do all of these psychologists work, and how much do they earn?

One outcome of the recent rapid growth of psychology is of interest: it is a profession of relatively young men and women. The stereotype of the gray-bearded professor practitioner is no longer, if it ever was, justified. Nearly one-third of the members of the American Psychological Association are younger than forty years of age, and most psychologists have earned their doctorates during the past twenty years.

Where the Jobs Are

Psychologists hold about 166,000 jobs. While many hold faculty positions at colleges and universities and as high school psychology teachers, educational institutions employ about 29 percent of psychologists in positions other than teaching, such as counseling, testing, research, and administration.

Academic psychologists today devote more time to research and to practice than in the past. More than a quarter of them also do some outside consulting work. Psychologists typically work about forty-five hours per week, and more than one-fifth work over fifty-five hours per week.

Private practice in clinical psychology on a full-time basis is the second-largest employment setting for doctoral psychologists. There are far more professional psychologists in private practice in large cities such as New York, Chicago, Toronto, Vancouver, and Los Angeles than ever before. Apparently the general increase in the demand for psychological services, along with changes in the opportunities for insurance reimbursement, have resulted in an increased demand for private consultation services. This need is also being met in part by academically employed psychologists who have a part-time clinical practice.

About 21 percent of psychologists are employed in health care, primarily in offices of mental health practitioners, hospitals, physicians' offices, and outpatient mental health and substance abuse centers. Government agencies at the state, provincial, and local levels employ psychologists in correctional facilities, law enforcement, and other settings.

Responses to the health care crisis that became a major focus of policy debate in the early 1990s continue to have a significant effect on psychologists in private practice and in hospitals and clinics. Under programs of managed care, such as health maintenance organizations and preferred provider organizations, there is a financial incentive for preventive care and early intervention. Psychologists have a central role in the mental health aspect of managed care, and they are often involved in evaluation and utilization studies, in which scientists and administrators track and analyze how patients use the services that are offered and whether these services are as efficient and effective as they should be.

Public schools and other nonprofit organizations also employ doctoral psychologists. Programs for the preparation of school psychologists now receive federal subsidies, as do clinical and counseling programs. Despite the surpluses of graduates in most teaching fields and the pressures on school budgets, specialties such as this still thrive, especially when they include competence in dealing with learning disabilities and high-level consulting skills.

Business and industry employ about 20 percent of doctoral-level psychologists. In fact, this is one area where job prospects are good for those with master's degrees who can find positions in survey design, analysis, and research to develop tools for marketing evaluation and statistical analysis.

Government agencies also employ about 10 percent of doctoral psychologists in agencies such as civil service commissions, departments of education, employment services, and departments of health and human services.

After several years of experience, some psychologists—usually those with doctoral degrees—enter private practice or set up private research or consulting firms. About 34 percent of psychologists were self-employed in 2006, compared with only 8 percent of all professional workers.

Diversity in Psychology

In a 2007 survey conducted by the APA Center for Psychology Workforce Analysis and Research, about 58 percent of the responding practitioners were women, up from 49.1 percent in 1999.

Ninety-three percent of respondents were white. Asians and Blacks each represented less than 2 percent of respondents, while just under 3 percent were Hispanic, followed by multiethnic at 0.6 percent and Native American at 0.3 percent.

Although the majority of both men and women reported working full-time, 44 percent of women indicated that they worked part-time, as opposed to 23 percent of men. Women were also more likely to be working in a single employment position than were men, at 72 percent and 67 percent, respectively.

While there were no substantive differences by race or ethnicity in working full-time, 69 percent of minorities reported being employed full-time, as opposed to 65 percent of white respondents. Respondents who were members of a minority group were slightly less apt to be working in a single position than were whites and were more apt to be working at two or more positions.

The top five employment settings for women were individual private practices, group psychological practices, private general hospitals, student counseling centers, and public general hospitals, accounting for 67 percent of female practitioners. At 69 percent, the top five settings for men were individual private practices, group psychological practices, primary care group practices, VA medical centers, and community mental health centers.

The top five employment settings for minority respondents, at 51 percent, were individual and group psychological practices, student counseling centers, VA medical centers, and primary care group practices. For whites, the top employment settings at 69 percent were individual and group practices, primary care group practices, private general hospitals, and VA medical centers.

The results of this survey indicate that although psychology is a profession open to all, minority groups are still underrepresented. Women have made significant strides in recent years, but the overwhelming numbers of white practitioners reveals that there is still a long way to go in order for psychology to become truly diverse.

To address this issue, the APA website offers useful information for psychology graduate students of diverse backgrounds. Topics are addressed to students of color; students with disabilities; lesbian, gay, bisexual, and transgender students; international students; and nontraditional students.

Compensation for Psychologists

The rewards of psychology are both tangible and intangible. Tangible rewards include earnings and the fringe benefits that go with them, such as housing, medical care, and retirement provisions. Intangible rewards include the satisfaction that comes with doing something that one likes, considers important, and that others value. Psychological studies of job satisfaction and morale have amply demonstrated the importance of both types of rewards.

Financial Rewards

The American Psychological Association conducts extensive salary surveys among its doctoral-level members. The salary range is wide and varies, depending on the work setting and number of years of experience. The new graduate working a nine-month contract at the bottom of the university hierarchy might start out at $42,000. At the top of the ladder salaries exceed $90,000; university researchers earn close to $100,000, and those in business and industry earn well over $100,000.

In general, salaries in the field of psychology compare well with those for chemists and engineers and are superior to those of social workers and teachers. Financially, psychologists are in the top 10 percent of the employed population.

Salary levels from the 2007 survey for doctoral-level psychologists working in different settings with various levels of experience are summarized in Table 4.1, and salary levels for master's degree holders appear in Table 4.2.

Table 4.1 Average Salaries of Doctoral-Level Psychologists (2007)

Position	Annual Median Salary
Academic Faculty	
Lecturer/instructor	$42,000
Assistant professor	$55,000
Associate professor	$66,000
Full professor	$95,000
Research Positions	
Private research	
2–4 years	$85,000
5–9 years	$80,000
10–14 years	$105,000
University psychology department	
2–4 years	$68,000
5–9 years	$65,000
University research center	
2–4 years	$59,000
5–9 years	$70,000
Government research	
2–4 years	$77,000
5–9 years	$84,000
Non-profit research	
5–9 years	$76,000
Direct Human Services—Clinical Psychology	
Elementary/secondary	
20–24 years	$90,000
Public general hospital	
5–9 years	$76,000
10–14 years	$82,000
Private general hospital	
5–9 years	$75,500
10–14 years	$78,000

(continued)

Table 4.1 Average Salaries of Doctoral-Level Psychologists (2007)
(continued)

Position	*Annual Median Salary*
VA hospital	
2–4 years	$76,000
5–9 years	$90,000
Individual private practice	
5–9 years	$87,000
10–14 years	$100,000
Group practice	
5–9 years	$73,000
10–14 years	$89,500
Direct Human Services—Counseling Psychology	
University/college counseling center	
5–9 years	$53,000
10–14 years	$62,000
VA hospital	
15–19 years	$95,000
Individual private practice	
5–9 years	$77,500
10–14 years	$60,000
15–19 years	$71,000
Group practice	
15–19 years	$55,000
Direct Human Services—School Psychology	
Elementary/secondary school	
2–4 years	$73,000
5–9 years	$72,000
School system district office	
2–4 years	$57,000
5–9 years	$73,500
Administration of Human Services	
University/college counseling center	
2–4 years	$67,000
5–9 years	$65,000
10–14 years	$80,000
Public general hospital	
25–29 years	$86,000

Private general hospital
    5–9 years $80,000
    10–14 years $90,000
VA hospital
    5–9 years $97,000
    10–14 years $93,000
Criminal justice system
    5–9 years $82,500
    10–14 years $91,000
Rehabilitation facility
    5–9 years $79,500

Applied Psychology—Industrial/Organizational

Consulting firm
    5–9 years $110,000
    10–14 years $91,000
    15–19 years $150,000
Business/industry
    5–9 years $95,000
    10–14 years $103,000
    15–19 years $147,000

Table 4.2 Average Starting Salaries of Full-Time Master's-Level Psychologists (2007)

Faculty positions	$38,000
Research positions	$36,000
Direct human services, clinical	$30,000
Direct human services, counseling	$33,000
Direct human services, school	$41,000
Administration of human services	$32,000
Applied psychology	$48,000

In 2007 doctoral-level psychologists who worked in business and industry—whether for a corporation or self-employed as a consultant—were the highest paid, along with clinical psychologists in private practice. The lowest paid were master's degree holders working in academic institutions. Ph.D.s also were paid the least in academic institutions.

Material rewards for psychologists vary with the type of organization. In private practice or consulting work, psychologists must provide themselves with retirement benefits, medical care, housing, and other necessities. They also will receive social security benefits after retirement. At the other extreme, psychologists commissioned in one of the armed forces have the benefits of medical care, retirement, housing, and commissary facilities traditionally available to military personnel. Colleges, hospitals, social agencies, school systems, and business and industry fall somewhere in between as to the type and number of benefits they provide. With respect to the nonsalary rewards, psychologists are just like physicians, engineers, lawyers, machinists, truck drivers, and janitors; what they receive depends on where they work.

Intangible Rewards

Now let's look at the intangible rewards, the work satisfaction, and the way of life that a psychologist enjoys. These fall into two categories: those that are associated with being a psychologist and those that are associated with working in institutions and organizations where psychologists are employed. Let's look at the former first, since it is more peculiar to psychology.

The work satisfaction of psychologists comes from the application of scientific methods to the understanding of human behavior and to the solution of problems of human relations and personal adjustment. Psychologists' work uniquely combines the methods of science and the subject matter of human relations. They are in a position to obtain the intellectual satisfaction of discovery, understanding, and invention at the same time that they experience the emotional satisfaction of working with and for people. Depending on the field of specialization, psychologists can emphasize or minimize the extent to which they do any one of these.

An experimental psychologist may have relatively brief and transient contacts with people in the course of work and may help people only indirectly. However, the experimental psychologist's intellectual satisfaction in understanding the principles of behavior, the development of theory, and the design of experiments and equipment may be great.

Clinical or counseling psychologists may combine the intellectual satisfaction of understanding the behavior of individuals and of exploring the many partially understood aspects of personality. They have the emotional satisfaction of helping people function more effectively and achieve self-fulfillment.

The research psychologist in a large organization, whether educational, industrial, military, or health-related, has the intellectual satisfaction derived from applying experimental methods to problems of the development and use of human resources. This is combined with the emotional satisfaction of making the people with whom he or she works more effective, thus contributing to the strength of our country's educational systems, economy, welfare, or defense.

The instructor in a college or university combines the intellectual satisfaction of organizing, sharing with others, and perhaps adding to the store of knowledge concerning human behavior, along with the emotional satisfaction of working with students and guiding their growth and early professional development.

Interviewing workers, teaching classes, planning statistical analyses, designing learning experiments, interpreting personality tests, reading research reports, writing texts, watching rats in a maze, teasing out the meanings of a variety of case materials, observing the behavior of children at play—these and the myriad other things psychologists do are time-consuming, often slow, sometimes tedious, rarely easy; but for many persons these can be thrilling activities.

To think up a neat and convincing design for an experiment that will put some theory to the test; to find the underlying trends that make the seemingly discordant elements of a client's personality form a meaningful whole; to help a patient or client develop more effective behavior patterns or find better outlets for his or her talents; to organize the findings of a number of discrete research studies into a chapter in a book that makes useful to others a new principle or an important diagnostic technique; to share with others the results of new research that has been well conceived and executed—these are deeply satisfying activities in which psychologists engage. They are exciting events when they happen, and they do not pall with age and experience. If anything, time makes them more enjoyable and more rewarding.

Psychologists enjoy a comfortable lifestyle. They may not have a wealth of material things, but neither do they suffer any hardship. Psychologists do not stand at the top of the social prestige ladder, but they are high enough to be respected by all and low enough to be acceptable to most. Their work brings them in contact with other educated persons with whom they can share the intellectual and aesthetic interests that usually develop during the course of college and graduate education. The psychologist's income is sufficient to indulge these interests, share them with neighbors, and rear children to appreciate and enjoy them.

Some Disadvantages

To present an honest picture, we should also consider the disadvantages of being a psychologist. But first, it bears asking the question, "advantages and disadvantages for whom?" It's an old saying that one person's meat is another person's poison, which means that you must ask yourself whether the type of work and the way of life described in this book is appealing to you, whether it will enable you to attain your goals, and whether it will provide the opportunity to be the kind of person you would like to be.

If you are more interested in the things that money will buy than in the things done to earn the money, you may find some disadvantages in psychology as a profession. While we have seen that psychologists earn as much as most professional groups, they earn less than people in other fields such as medicine and the higher levels of business, and the work is intellectually and often emotionally demanding.

You may also find that there are certain drawbacks associated with the type of institution or enterprise in which you work. In an educational institution, you might have too little clerical assistance. In a psychiatric hospital or school for the mentally retarded, your patients or students might present demands that leave you feeling emotionally exhausted.

If you work in a business organization at the technician level, your day might be similar to that of an administrative clerk. If you hold a position of leadership, your work will be closer to that of an executive. In the first case, you might feel underappreciated; in the second, you may experience pressure to keep up with colleagues' lifestyles. As a behavioral scientist, you might consider such competition superficial and perhaps unhealthy, although some view it simply as a necessary game one must play in order to succeed.

The work satisfaction and way of life associated with working in the organizations where psychologists find employment are not peculiar to the field. Psychologists who work in schools share many of the satisfactions, problems, and ways of life of teachers. Those who work in hospitals share satisfaction and problems similar to those of physicians, nurses, occupational therapists, and others who also work there. Psychologists who work in colleges or graduate schools share the work satisfaction and living conditions common to college professors. Those who work in business in many ways resemble businessmen and businesswomen, for they share their work and their social lives, even while maintaining a professional identity.

In choosing the type of organization in which to work, the psychologist also chooses the type of community in which to live, the friends with whom to associate, the kind of home to have, and the children with whom his or her children will grow up and go to school.

5

PLANNING A CAREER
IN PSYCHOLOGY

Now THAT YOU know about psychology as a profession and the educational and training requirements you must fulfill to become a psychologist, how do you start to plan your career in this field?

According to vocational psychologists, a career is not an occupation; it is a sequence of positions held by a person. Careers exist only in the lives of individuals, beginning with education and the occupation of the student and continuing with work and the occupation of a sequence of positions that may or may not be substantively related. So a career in architecture may begin with earning the appropriate degrees and working as a draftsperson, acceptance into an established firm, promotion to senior architect, and recognition as partner.

In this chapter, we will consider what it takes to get started, get ahead, and keep up in psychology.

Getting Started

If you aspire to a profession, you should know what the profession is, what sort of work it entails, where the work is done, what the future prospects are for the field, what kind of training you will need to enter the profession, and where to get this training. In addition, you also must know how to get started and become established in your chosen profession. Most of these issues, such as job analysis and description, social and economic trends, and training are relatively objective and easily dealt with. But getting started and getting established in a profession is another matter. It is a social and psychological process with many variations and is much more difficult to observe and to analyze.

It is not uncommon for people to be reluctant to look at their jobs objectively, because they may prefer not to consider both the negative and positive aspects. And in many cases, such an exercise leads to a personal evaluation that may be equally unsettling. In order to successfully plan a career, however, you need to be honest about yourself and your abilities and aspirations.

Personal Evaluation

As a student of psychology who is about to complete formal professional education, whether at the M.A. or Ph.D. level, you will be a merchandiser about to put a new product on the market—yourself in the form of your professional services. You have to analyze your product to see what there is about it that people might want and determine how to get it to that market in the most attractive way.

To conduct this analysis, you should review all of your educational and vocational experiences to see what you can offer in the way of psychological services that other people want. What assets do you have, as a teacher, researcher, clinician, counselor, or administrator? Have you worked as a graduate assistant with teaching responsibilities? If so, this is a vocational asset. Was the teaching assistantship in association with a psychologist who had a strong reputation as a teacher? If the answer is yes, perhaps you caught some of the sponsor's inspiration, and this, too, is an asset. Did you participate in any research activities independent of your thesis? These should be considered as a sign of the breadth of your experience, originality, and research ability. Were these research activities carried on in collaboration with a well-known research psychologist, and did they result in publication? Did you complete an internship in a clinic or research institute with a reputation for high standards and good work? Did you win the esteem of supervisors and colleagues during this internship? These are all points that may have market value. Did you participate in any nonpsychological activities that might show creative ability, leadership, or culture? These things are valued in college teachers, research workers, clinicians, and administrators.

The purpose of listing assets is, of course, to examine them to see to whom they might be of value and how. They may point up college teaching (the successful teaching assistant), public school work (the former teacher), market research (the former business major), research on international communication (the social psychologist who spent time in the Far East), or counseling in a community agency (the homemaker who raised a family, was active in the PTA, and served on social agency boards). As a student, hopefully you have planned your education and training with a special market in mind so that when you prepare to seek a position, you will do so with knowledge of both yourself and the market.

Once you have analyzed your training and experience, it's time to survey the job market. You may locate potential positions by reviewing items in professional journals such as the *American Psychologist* and the APA *Monitor*. The websites of both the American Psychological Association (www.apa.org) and the Canadian Psychological Association (www.cpa.ca) offer career information and list job openings. You can also look through the listings in newspapers and talk with faculty members, practicum supervisors, and friends about employment possibilities.

It is also a good idea to consider recent developments that may have had an impact on the field of psychology. For example, the continuing needs of military personnel returning from deployment in Iraq require the services of psychologists skilled in dealing with post-traumatic stress disorder, severe physical and emotional trauma, and occupational and rehabilitation needs. The unfortunate occurrence of violence in schools presents a need for specialists in childhood and adolescent psychology to help students deal with their fears. An uncertain economy may spur an increase in the need for psychologists to work with clients whose jobs have been downsized or outsourced. And our ever-aging population makes the services of gerontologists quite valuable.

The proliferation of community colleges means that more teachers, counselors, and deans will be required. The growing number of social programs adds to the demand for educational, social, counseling, and measurement psychologists. The rapid growth of human services has prepared openings for large numbers of psychologists providing health services.

You can make yourself available in a variety of ways, some subtle, some obvious, all appropriate in their proper places. Some of the ways consist of publishing minor research and reading papers at psychological meetings while you are still a student; taking on short-term and vacation jobs that bring you into contact with potential employers and with people who know employers; attending professional meetings and taking advantage of the occasional opportunities that arise to increase your acquaintances among psychologists; and getting to know the members of your own department as well as possible so that you will be thought of when openings are available.

One psychologist employed in a large-scale research program was offered his position because a paper he read at a national convention as a graduate student caught the attention of the psychologist who later headed up the research program. Another obtained her position as a college professor because, at another convention, she dined with a friend who was sitting with a third psychologist who was looking for a new assistant professor. Still another psychologist is director of a college counseling center because he accepted a minor assistantship while a graduate student, and he carried out his routine duties in a way that made him stand out in the minds of the faculty as a person of unusual ability. Finally, a young woman in the male-dominated field of industrial psychology got her start in industry by working on a professor's research, which took her into several business organizations.

Placement Services

Registering with a placement service is a very acceptable method of making yourself available to employers. Most universities operate placement offices where you can find information about job openings. Many faculty members operate informal placement services, keeping lists or résumés of students and former students interested in jobs. Some professors, research workers, and practitioners receive many requests for nominations to jobs from employers who know them or their work. Having papers on file in the placement office makes it easy for a professor to recommend someone with supporting evidence.

The American Psychological Association operates a placement service, listing positions available and positions wanted in a monthly employment section of the APA *Monitor*, which is sent to all members and to many libraries. The *Observer* of the American Psychological Society also lists employment openings. Large professional meetings, such as the annual national convention of the American Psychological Association, also provide placement services and facilitate interviews. The state employment offices in some states operate placement services for psychologists in their professional divisions. Finally, federal, state, and provincial civil service examinations offer another means for psychologists in search of employment. There often are openings in the federal civil service for research psychologists with physiological, experimental, social, psychometric, personnel, clinical, and counseling specialties.

Résumés, Applications, and Personal Interviews

Whichever method you use to find a job, you will need a résumé to present to potential employers. The résumé should include your education and experience and be designed to show your suitability for a certain type of employment.

The main route to applying for a job is to send your résumé and cover letter in response to an advertisement for a position, whether from a newspaper, professional journal, website, or placement office.

Your résumé is an important introduction to the potential employer; it will be the first impression that you make. Be sure to follow any instructions for submission, such as sending a résumé electronically or by fax, if that is requested.

There are many books available that can lead you through the steps of preparing a résumé and cover letter. Some job search websites, such as Monster.com and CareerBuilder.com, provide assistance as well. You may also ask at your school's career guidance office if assistance is available.

In addition, you may find books designed to help you with mastering the personal interview. While there are certain aspects of the job interview that apply to all professions, there are specific customs in the employment of psychologists that you should be aware of. For example, colleges and universities like to observe certain protocol, even though they may actually engage in hard-headed bargaining. Most major universities won't put themselves in the position of being turned down by a candidate for employment. They sometimes achieve this by asking the candidate, late in the interview process, whether he or she would accept the position if offered a specific salary.

The colleges expect that applicants will also be above bargaining. You can achieve this by knowing ahead of time what salary you can command and what salary the college is likely willing to pay. You can also let the college know in various subtle ways that you know what you are worth. The university is likely to offer a position only if it has been led by its own analysis to believe that what it is interested in paying is what you believe you are worth or feel forced by circumstances to accept.

The hiring processes in medical, social work, governmental, and industrial settings are different in some respects from those in colleges and universities. They are generally more formalized; salaries in governmental organizations are more predetermined, and in business, they're more negotiable.

A Good Beginning

Getting off to a good start in your new position, like applying for the job, requires a knowledge of and respect for ways of doing things. The psychologist working in governmental or industrial bureaucracy must know the official channels through which business is conducted. The college instructor must be able to see a challenge rather than an insult in the immaturity of some of the students. And each type of situation has its dress code, be it a business suit, lab coat, or blue jeans.

The undergraduate student may have limited horizons and lack intellectual curiosity. The business executive may be interested in answers that give results rather than in methods that give answers. The military officer may desire results immediately if not sooner. The patient may refuse to conform to textbook types. The medical specialist may have more confidence in the conclusions that he or she reaches after working with one case than in those that someone else drew from a statistical analysis of one hundred cases. These are just a few of the more serious and constant challenges that the newly employed psychologist must accept graciously and learn to handle to keep the job and render the type of service that will make the job worth keeping.

Getting Ahead

Once you have started your new job and made the initial adjustments to become part of the institution in which you work, the next challenge you'll face is that of getting ahead. You will most likely stay in that first position for one or two years, to demonstrate your stability and dependability. At the same time, you should plan some activities that will pave the way for promotion or for offers of better positions. If you plan wisely, doing justice to the job, to the profession, and to the public, you will also add to your professional stature. For example, like other scientists and professional people, as a psychologist you will have a responsibility for keeping up with new developments in the field. The rapid progress being made by psychology makes this a real chore; the volume of newly published research is great. It is your responsibility to read, interpret, and apply this new knowledge at work.

The means most typically used by psychologists to bring about advancement are teaching, writing, research, practice (application), professional activity (committee work and office holding), and popularization. These are not all equally effective or equally esteemed, but all are used.

Teaching

In a field that includes both pure and applied science, university connections and university teaching confer prestige. Universities seek faculty members who have excelled in some aspect of their scientific or professional work. These are the psychologists who have something to contribute to students, who will attract new students, and who will in other ways help build up the institution.

The prestige of university connections makes part-time teaching appointments a means by which psychologists working in clinics, hospitals, counseling centers, schools, industry, and government agencies advance in their fields. Those who can teach others to do what they have done well add to their professional stature and make themselves known to a larger audience of psychologists and other consumers of psychological knowledge. They make their wisdom and skill known in a highly acceptable way. They also enjoy sharing their knowledge with interested students.

Psychologists who are full-time instructors or professors are in a position to build strong reputations as teachers. They are able to organize and conduct courses in such a way as to attract students who will want to study with them because their instruction is meaningful and helpful. In some institutions it may be that attracting large numbers is important, for numbers mean fees and financial support to poorly endowed institutions. In others, it is not so much quantity as quality that counts, and the teacher who attracts outstanding students who make their mark on the field is the teacher who comes over time to be valued. Such instructors get recognition and advancement when other universities and institutions bid for their services and when their own institutions try to keep them.

Good teaching does not just happen, and good teachers are not all good in the same way. The ability to synthesize and interpret the knowledge of your field, both theory and research, is an important component. The ability to present knowledge, whether in lectures, projects, or other less traditional ways, also is an important quality in teaching.

Although you may master the substance of your field in graduate school, the ability to teach is too often not developed in doctoral programs. It also isn't necessarily something you can pick up through observation. As a graduate student, you will be graded on your command of the substance and methodology of the field, not on your ability to teach.

If you aspire to be a teacher of psychology, pay attention to how your professors teach. Look for opportunities to assist in teaching, and welcome suggestions and criticisms of your performance with an eye to improvement. Psychologists who win distinction as teachers do so only with some effort and after a period of unofficial internship in teaching, including their first years as teachers. Obtaining class evaluations provides helpful material, especially if you recognize that good teaching for one student may not be good teaching for another. The evaluation of fellow instructors also can be helpful.

The ability to synthesize and present in the classroom or laboratory can contribute to your reputation not only on the campus but beyond it. Some of the best and most widely used textbooks have been produced by instructors who developed their own materials, tried them out on their own students, improved them with field trials, and then published them with eventual national recognition.

However, superior teaching, important as it is to colleges and universities, often is not enough to bring advancement. A teacher's reputation generally does not spread rapidly, and when it does spread, it is in quiet ways that may not come immediately to the attention of administrators. Unless offers from other institutions are forthcoming, good teaching brings promotion slowly.

Publication

Publication, on the other hand—whether in the form of textbooks, research monographs, articles in professional and scientific journals, or papers at scientific meetings—attracts attention more rapidly. It is tangible, and its results can be brought together and examined for quantity and quality. A study that is frequently quoted in textbooks, a text that is used in many institutions, or even a number of journal articles that may have limited intrinsic value, have the effect of publicizing both the author and the institution where the psychologist works.

Once a psychologist becomes well known through publication, this reputation attracts students, clients, grants, contracts, offers of positions, and promotions. For academic psychologists, those in research positions, and those employed in medical, community, governmental, or industrial settings, this is a superior and satisfying way in which to develop a reputation among other psychologists and among kindred professionals and executives.

Research

Research is closely related to publication as a means of advancement. Research usually will result in publication, but it is different in some respects. Developing a reputation as a writer may be achieved through textbooks, reviews, or other contributions not based on original research or experimentation. Research may lead only to rare monographs, articles, and papers, but it may be so important that its impact is great. The nature and scope of a project may capture the imagination of others. Its planning may be so well conceived and its initial stages so well carried out that the psychologists involved in the project will acquire reputations as research workers even before any significant publications result from their work.

The emphasis on scientific method and the interest in functioning as a scientific profession that characterize modern psychology tend to make research and writing a critical component for establishing a reputation and for advancing in the field. They are methods that are very satisfying to an intellectually curious, research-minded person.

Development Work

The practice of psychology is another means of advancement that has become increasingly important as the demand for psychological services increases and as the number of psychological practitioners grows. Engineering, industrial-organizational, measurement, school, counseling, or applied social psychologists who are especially effective in development work in business, the armed forces, or education find their services very much in demand.

The term *development* may need a little explanation. It frequently is used in connection with the term *research*. The development of a proficiency examination for police officers or for computer programmers, for example, is not research in the strict sense of the word. It involves no new contributions to knowledge but is simply the application of existing techniques to a different situation. It is, however, a task best carried out or supervised by those with a research background and research skills.

Similarly, making a follow-up study of students who have left high school, in order to get data for use in revising the offerings of the school, involves no new techniques and contributes no new fundamental knowledge. It is, again, the kind of project to which a research-trained educational, industrial-organizational, or counseling psychologist can contribute a great deal in rationale, method, and interpretation.

A number of consulting organizations and research institutes specialize in this type of work, and many college teachers are active consultants on such projects. Those who are skillful in working with others to put existing knowledge to work find themselves valued as staff members and as consultants, and thus they become established rapidly.

Clinical and Counseling Work

The practice of psychology is not limited to development work. In fact, it is the clinical and counseling applications of psychology that traditionally have been best known. They, too, are very much in demand; as a result, competent clinicians and counselors have found ample opportunity to advance to responsible positions or to develop private practices.

The practicing clinical or counseling psychologist may build a reputation partly through publication, research, and teaching, but in practice these are incidental or peripheral activities. Their principal functions are diagnosis, assessment, psychotherapy, and counseling. The practitioner therefore develops a reputation among professional colleagues and among clients by establishing and maintaining good interpersonal relations, by becoming a skillful diagnostician, by doing an effective job of counseling or psychotherapy, and by communicating with colleagues in psychology and in the related professions in ways that are meaningful to them.

The practitioners' services are valued because social workers find that their case summaries provide a sound and clear basis for child placement. Pediatricians find them good team members in working with difficult children and parents. Psychiatrists find their diagnostic summaries perceptive and to the point. And teachers feel that practitioners understand school problems and help show how classroom situations can be used to help children. It is those who are effective in this type of work who are offered opportunities for supervisory and administrative responsibility.

Committee Work

Committee work often proves to be an important means of highlighting a psychologist's ability and contributions. This is especially true in the case of teachers whose superior teaching builds reputations rather slowly, and in the case of clinicians and counselors whose effective work with clients and professional colleagues may remain known only in the relatively limited circles of their institutions. The American Psychological Association, the American Psychological Society, the Canadian Psychological Association, and the various state and provincial psychological associations have a large number of active committees working on a variety of scientific and professional problems. The burden of committee work falls heavily on those who have the ability and the motivation to work, so that new talent is regularly and eagerly sought and soon given responsibility.

Popularization

Popularization (disseminating psychology for the general public, whether in print, in speech, or online) is another method sometimes used by psychologists to build reputations and to advance careers. Traditionally, however, the profession as a whole has not viewed this very favorably, unless it is incidental to substantive contributions or done by professional writers. Psychology has a strong popular appeal, which creates a demand for popularization in widely read magazines, popular books, newspaper stories, the Internet, radio, television, and public lectures. The very nature of the appeal, however, often results in the distortion of psychological data, selection of the sensational, and catering to unhealthy needs and interests.

Popularization that is in the public interest requires much skill, time, and strength of mind on the part of the psychologist. Many have found their best efforts frustrated by a sales-minded publisher or TV producer, and some have violated the APA's code of ethics by succumbing to easy money through popular writing and lecturing that has led them to cater to publicity and sales departments.

Another important factor is the tendency of scientists to be skeptical of popularizers, even though it is in the interest of a science or a profession to have its work understood and supported by the public. The American Psychological Association, the American Psychological Society, and the Canadian Psychological Association are aware of the need for good popularization, and publishers, press, radio, and television are receptive to it. There is growing interest in psychology for these media, which may appeal to some psychologists with the writing skills and ethical standards to do the job well.

Networking

Achieving something better is almost an innate part of our modern psyche. Moving from one place to another, from one job to another, even from one occupation to another often has been viewed as the means to this end. Even those of us who really like our jobs sometimes make changes in order to advance our positions.

Mobility is not always a necessity, but having other employers want to hire you often does help to make you seem valued at your own institution or organization. The potential of mobility is good, provided it doesn't make you restless and distracted from the work at hand. We have already covered the means of making yourself wanted in the job market; in the next section, we'll consider the types of mobility that are typical of psychologists.

Academic Networks

Each graduate school has its network of communicating, mutually respecting, and accepting institutions. The foundations of these networks are partly geographic, because people from neighboring institutions meet more readily, for example, at the annual regional American Psychological Association meetings. They are partly affiliational, because people tend to maintain contact with their former professors, their fellow alumni, and their own former students. And they are partly hierarchical—prestige-based—because the famous universities tend to place their graduates in other well-known institutions, and the universities with local reputations, no matter how good, tend to place their graduates in nearby, sometimes lesser, institutions.

You will find that there are several academic networks, and movement tends to be within the network in which you start your academic work. People do move from higher-level networks to lower, sometimes because of the attractions of less famous but in other ways very attractive colleges or universities, or sometimes because of the lack of openings in the favored network. Movement from a lower-level network to a higher one is less common and is most likely to be the result of unusually good research or writing. This is less often the case in the applied fields, where it may be the result of unusual contributions in the development of service programs or in professional committee work.

Some graduate schools make a practice of employing their best graduates in junior positions after they get their degrees—which helps in getting teaching experience—while others prefer to see them go elsewhere and prove their worth in the field before considering them for teaching appointments. Those who stay at their alma mater too often have a rude awakening when they are pushed out of the nest after four or five years of service to make room for a newer candidate for whom tenure will not be a question for several years. The possibilities of getting tenure are important in considering a first regular academic appointment, and getting onto a tenure track at least one or two years after receiving a graduate degree generally is wise in academia.

Practitioner Networks

Careers in private practice may, of course, involve consultation either with individuals (clinical or counseling) or organizations (industrial and organizational, including assessment, counseling, and organizational and group development). Practitioners may work alone or in groups. It is clinicians and counselors who are most likely to eventually work on their own with private patients or clients, while some, like most industrial and organizational psychologists who engage in consulting work, do so within an organizational framework.

The common pattern for starting a career as a practitioner is to begin in a junior staff position in an institutional or organizational setting, partly to develop expertise and partly to accumulate evidence of legitimacy and competence. This is a good way to develop competence and contacts, as well as the maturity and confidence you will need to further your career. You can then move to full-time practice on your own or in higher-level organizational work.

Reputations as practitioners develop largely through word of mouth, personal contacts, training workshops, and work well done. Getting ahead will be determined first by the type of work that you are assigned. Then it will be determined by the types of problems on which you are asked to consult and on the volume of work or business that you develop, whether within the framework of an organization or on your own.

It may at first seem odd that clinical and industrial practice are dealt with together, as they are here. The reason lies not only in the fact that both are applied fields but also because people in either clinical or industrial practice do need to start in an institutional setting, unless they can take a gamble for some time while building a practice from scratch. The networks are distinct, but their patterns are similar.

Think Tanks, Research Institutes, and Freelance Work

A small but growing number of psychologists conduct research outside the academic setting in think tanks or research institutes, such as the American Institutes for Research, the Canadian Policy Research Network, or freelancing on their own. Such work is similar in many ways to academic research, often resulting in professional publication as well as a final report to the client (a government funding agency, a private foundation that supports research, or perhaps a business firm). Usually the research is directed to specific problems in the nonacademic world.

In many ways, however, psychologists in these networks forge careers that resemble those of practitioners; their work is oriented to a "product" rather than teaching and pure knowledge, and their networks of colleagues and potential employers again are distinct. This group of hybrid occupations has emerged for a variety of economic and structural reasons and is still in the process of defining its niche between the academic and the traditional practice.

You will find that linkages among the academic, practitioner, and research networks are limited once you have completed your university studies and may be of little help to you. If you are an academic psychologist whose work (research, writing, or teaching) brings you to the notice of business, industry, institutes, or government, you may be able to make contributions to practice by developing part-time consulting work; you may even find yourself in a position to receive or seek job offers. An occasional practitioner (whether clinical, counseling, or industrial-organizational) or researcher may be offered an academic post so that students can have the benefit of one or more full-time professors with strong applied backgrounds. But such instances are exceptional.

The higher incomes of successful practitioners do sometimes tempt the academics. Conversely, the greater security of the academic world sometimes tempts the psychologist in business or industry. The greater freedom of university work may tempt the industrial, business, or government employee or other practitioner who feels tied down by office hours. Or the risks, challenges, and real-world experience of applied work may tempt the teacher or professor tired of the grind of grading papers and lecturing. Each person considering a career in psychology should take into account that this great variety of options is available and that what is a wise choice for one person may not be a wise choice for another. Explore the possibilities while you are still in college and graduate school so that you can plan your graduate program to best qualify you for your desired type of career in psychology.

6

SCIENTIFIC AND PROFESSIONAL ORGANIZATIONS IN PSYCHOLOGY

FOR MORE THAN one hundred years, the primary professional and scientific association for psychologists in North America has been the American Psychological Association (APA). In the past three decades, more and more Canadian psychologists have joined the Canadian Psychological Association (CPA). There are a number of smaller, more narrowly focused associations, such as the Psychonomic Society, and many psychologists also belong to related professional societies such as the American Educational Research Association—some of these are listed later in this chapter.

The Association for Psychological Science (APS), formerly the American Psychological Society, was formed largely by members of the APA who were unhappy with what they perceived as a slighting of scientific concerns in favor of professional or health provider issues. The APS has grown rapidly and developed a number of new activities. At the same time, the APA has responded innovatively to many of the criticisms from academic psychologists and has maintained its high level of professional representation in the public sphere, especially with regard to health care policy reform. Many psychologists are members of both organizations.

American Psychological Association

The American Psychological Association has its headquarters in Washington, DC. In addition, it maintains an extensive website at www.apa.org. There you'll find information on the APA and its divisions as well as information on the following.

Accredited schools/programs
Boards and committees
Books
Careers
Conferences
Continuing education
Conventions
International affairs
Jobs
Journals
Licensure
Pamphlets
Position papers
Publications and communications
Research funding
Research office
Salary surveys
State associations

But that doesn't even scratch the surface. A visit to the APA website is a must for any potential psychology major.

The APA is a large organization with a staff that includes administrative professionals, editors and editorial assistants for its journals, communications specialists, project managers, accountants, sales managers, and many others concerned with professional education and placement. Its affairs are directed by an elected president, other officers, and a board of directors. In addition, there is a larger council of representatives elected by the various divisions of the association. Much of the association's work is carried out by boards and committees, some of which are listed here.

Board of Directors
Agenda Planning Group
American Psychological Association of Graduate Students
    Committee
College of Professional Psychology
Commission for the Recognition of Specialties and
    Proficiencies in Professional Psychology
Committee for the Advancement of Professional Practice
Committee on Division/APA Relations
Committee on Employment and Human Resources
Committee on International Relations in Psychology
Election Committee
Ethics Committee
Finance Committee
Investment Committee
Membership Committee
Public Information Committee

*Board for the Advancement of Psychology
in the Public Interest*
Committee on Aging
Committee on Disability Issues in Psychology
Committee on Children, Youth, and Families
Committee on Ethnic Minority Affairs
Committee on Lesbian, Gay, and Bisexual Concerns
Committee on Urban Initiatives
Committee on Women in Psychology

Board of Educational Affairs
Committee on Accreditation
Committee for the Approval of Continuing Education
    Sponsors
Committee of Teachers of Psychology in Secondary
    Schools

Board of Scientific Affairs
Committee on Animal Research and Ethics
Committee on Psychological Tests and Assessments
Committee on Scientific Affairs

Board of Professional Affairs
Committee on Professional Practice and Standards

Publications and Communications Board
Council of Editors

The special-interests APA members are served by the divisions
listed in Chapter 2. Each division is concerned either with a special

aspect of psychology as a science, with the applications of psychology in some special field, or with the interests of psychologists employed in a particular type of setting.

Members of the American Psychological Association may be either members or associates. Members have a doctoral degree in psychology or a related field from a regionally accredited graduate or professional school, or from a school that achieved such accreditation within five years of the doctoral degree (or a school of similar standing outside of the United States). Associates have a master's degree or have completed two years of graduate study in psychology or a related field at a regionally accredited institution. Degrees from foreign institutions must show U.S. equivalency.

Additional categories of membership are student affiliate, for graduate or undergraduate students taking courses in psychology; high school affiliate, for high school students who are interested in a career in psychology or want to see what it's all about; high school teacher affiliate, which allows teachers of high school psychology to join the APA; community college teacher affiliate, for teachers of psychology at community colleges; and international affiliate, for psychologists who live outside the United States and Canada.

In addition to the national association, there are regional, state, and provincial associations that meet regularly to hear scientific papers, to discuss problems of common interest, and occasionally to take action on professional matters. Most of these associations limit their activities to one meeting each year.

There are many benefits of APA membership. The association provides such services as insurance programs, financial services, education loans and student loan consolidation, discounts on computers and electronics, electronic payment processing, and career services.

Visit the website at www.apa.org for complete information on membership, current dues, conventions, and a wealth of other useful information.

Association for Psychological Science

The large increase in membership of the American Psychological Association in the last two decades is largely a result of the rapid growth of psychologists providing health services. But the growth and particularly the shift toward psychology as a health profession created great tensions within the association about how best to organize its affairs for promoting both the science and the practice of psychology. As a result, a large number of psychologists formed the American Psychological Society, now called the Association for Psychological Science. Many of these psychologists were based in university or research institutions and were oriented to the science side of psychology, although many of them had applied, if not clinical, interests as well. A large number maintain membership in both organizations.

The Association for Psychological Science was founded in 1988 and now has more than eighteen thousand members. It currently publishes four journals: *Psychological Science*, which carries articles on research, theory, and applications in psychology and related behavioral, cognitive, neural, and social sciences; *Current Directions in Psychological Science,* which features summaries and reviews of recent trends and controversies in a manner that is accessible to a wider audience of readers both within and outside the discipline; *Psychological Science in the Public Interest*, which features assessments of topics where psychological science may have the potential to improve the well-being of society, such as the impact of classroom size on student achievement and whether herbal supplements can enhance cognitive abilities; and *Perspectives on Psychological Science*, which presents theoretical statements, literature reviews, viewpoints and opinions, research presentations, and scholarship. The APS also publishes a monthly newsletter, the *Observer*.

There is an annual meeting of the society, at which numerous symposia and reports of scientific studies are presented. It also provides advocacy for members in such areas as education and research.

In addition to regular membership, graduate student affiliate and undergraduate student affiliate membership is open to anyone currently enrolled in a degree program in psychology or a related field at an accredited institution.

Visit www.psychologicalscience.org for complete information.

Canadian Psychological Association

The Canadian Psychological Association (CPA) was organized in 1939 and incorporated in 1950. With a membership of six thousand, the CPA is comprised of the following divisions:

Aboriginal Psychology
Adult Development and Aging
Brain and Behaviour
Clinical Neuropsychology
Clinical Psychology
Community Psychology
Counseling Psychology
Criminal Justice Psychology
Developmental Psychology
Environmental Psychology

Family Psychology
Health Psychology
History and Philosophy of Psychology
Industrial and Organizational Psychology
International and Cross-Cultural Psychology
Perception, Learning, and Cognition
Psychoanalytic and Psychodynamic Psychology
Psychologists in Education
Psychology in the Military
Psychology and Religion
Psychopharmacology
Rural and Northern Psychology
Sexual Orientation and Gender Identity Issues
Social and Personality Psychology
Sport and Exercise Psychology
Students in Psychology
Substance Abuse/Dependence
Teaching of Psychology
Traumatic Stress
Women and Psychology

The association sponsors four regular publications. The journal *Canadian Psychology* publishes general articles of interest to psychologists; the *Canadian Journal of Behavioural Science* is the only social science journal for the field in Canada; and the *Canadian Journal of Experimental Psychology* is the nation's only journal in its area. The Canadian Psychological Association also publishes a quarterly newspaper, *Psynopsis.*

The annual convention includes presentation of papers, workshops, business meetings, awards presentations, and opportunities for networking and looking for jobs.

Visit the CPA website at www.cpa.ca for information on membership, advocacy, and much more.

American Board of Professional Psychology

The American Board of Professional Psychology is appointed from a list of leading psychologists nominated by the American Psychological Association. The board is a separately incorporated entity responsible for examining and certifying psychologists in the professional fields and issuing diplomas in clinical, counseling, industrial, and school psychology.

Diplomates, as the recipients of these diplomas are called, must have held a doctorate in psychology with appropriate specialization for at least five years. In addition, they must have experience in their specialty, meet high ethical standards, and pass written, oral, and practical examinations in the general field of psychology and in their specialty.

Certification by the board serves the public interest by making it easier to identify practicing psychologists who are clearly recognized by their fellows as having attained a high level of competence and who have adhered to high levels of ethical standards. The publication of a directory of approved psychological service centers is the function of the American Board of Professional Psychology. Several other boards exist for special purposes.

Complete information about the board and a directory of specialists are available at www.abpp.org.

Psi Chi

Psi Chi is the national honor society in psychology with chapters on the campuses of more than one thousand colleges and universities in North America. It holds meetings like those of the state and local associations and helps with the orientation of psychology students to their field, but its main purpose is to encourage students to maintain excellence in psychology and advance the science of psychology.

Membership is open to undergraduate and graduate students in psychology who meet certain minimum requirements. Students become members by joining the chapter at the school where they are enrolled. Individual chapters are operated by student officers and faculty advisors who select and induct the members and carry out the goals of the society.

The society publishes a quarterly magazine, *Eye on Psi Chi*, which recognizes members' contributions and accomplishments. The quarterly *Psi Chi Journal of Undergraduate Research* publishes papers written by undergraduate psychology students. For more information about activities and membership, go to www.psichi.org.

Related Associations

There are a number of other scientific and professional societies that include psychological divisions or in which psychologists and members of related fields meet. These include the following.

American Association for the Advancement of Science
American Association on Intellectual and Developmental Disabilities
American Educational Research Association
American Management Association
American Orthopsychiatric Association
American Personnel and Guidance Association

Association for the Advancement of Psychology
International Association of Applied Psychology
International Association for Cross-Cultural Psychology
International Society of Political Psychology
National Association of School Psychologists
National Education Association
Psychonomic Society

State and Provincial Licensing and Certification Boards

Psychologists in independent practice or those who offer any type of patient care—including clinical, counseling, and school psychologists—must meet certification or licensing requirements in all states and provinces. Licensing laws vary by jurisdiction and by type of position. They require licensed or certified psychologists to limit their practice to areas in which they have developed professional competence through training and experience. Clinical and counseling psychologists usually need a doctorate in psychology, an approved internship, and one to two years of professional experience. In addition, all locations require that applicants pass an examination. Most licensing boards administer a standardized test, and many supplement that with additional oral or essay questions. Some states require continuing education for renewal of the license.

The Association of State and Provincial Psychology Boards (ASPPB) sponsors the Examination for Professional Practice in Psychology (EPPP), which is used by licensing boards to assess candidates for licensure and certification. Visit the association's website at www.asppb.org for information on licensure, on the EPPP, and for a listing of doctoral and postdoctoral programs.

The National Association of School Psychologists (NASP) awards the Nationally Certified School Psychologist (NCSP) designation in the United States and Canada, which recognizes professional competency in school psychology at a national rather than state level. Requirements for the NCSP include the completion of sixty graduate semester hours in school psychology; a twelve-hundred-hour internship, six hundred hours of which must be completed in a school setting; and a passing score on the National School Psychology Examination. Detailed information is available at www.nasp.org.

The American Board of Professional Psychology (ABPP) recognizes professional achievement by awarding specialty certification in thirteen different areas. Candidates for ABPP certification need a doctorate in psychology, postdoctoral training in their specialty, several years of experience, and professional endorsements, and they are required to pass the specialty board examination. For more information, visit www.abpp.org.

National Register of Health Service Providers in Psychology

The National Register credentials licensed psychologists in the United States and Canada and helps make the public aware of these professionals. To qualify for the National Register Health Service Providers in Psychology credential, a psychologist must have a doctoral degree from an ASPPB/National Register–designated doctoral program in psychology or an APA/CPA accredited program; at least two years (three thousand hours) of supervised experience in health services; an active, unrestricted license at the independent practice level; and no disciplinary action. For the most current information on credentialing issues, go to its website www.nationalregister.org. The National Register offers continuing education credits that can be completed online. Continuing education is divided into modules, each of which contains a series of selected articles from past issues of *The Register Report*, the National Register's semiannual publication. Go to www.e-psychologist.org for complete information.

Consumers and patients can use the National Register website to locate qualified psychologists in all states and provinces. Visit www.findapsychologist.org to search more than twelve thousand psychologists, read information on various topics in psychology, as well as find links to current news articles that address issues in the field.

North American Psychology Licensing Boards

Following is the contact information for every state and provincial licensing board. Websites are given where available.

United States

Alabama

Alabama Board of Examiners in Psychology
660 Adams Ave., Ste. 360
Montgomery, AL 36104
www.psychology.state.al.us

Alaska

Alaska Board of Psychologist and Psychological Associate Examiners
333 Willoughby Ave., 9th Fl.
Juneau, AK 99811
www.dced.state.ak.us/occ/ppsy.htm

Arizona

Arizona Board of Psychologist Examiners
1400 W. Washington, Rm. 235
Phoenix, AZ 85007
www.psychboard.az.gov

Arkansas

Arkansas Board of Psychology
101 E. Capitol, Ste. 415
Little Rock, AR 72201
www.state.ar.us/abep

California

California Board of Psychology
1422 Howe Ave., Ste. 22
Sacramento, CA 95825
www.psychboard.ca.gov

Colorado

Colorado Board of Psychologist Examiners
1560 Broadway, Ste. 880
Denver, CO 80202
www.dora.state.co.us/mental-health

Connecticut

Connecticut Board of Examiners of Psychologists
Department of Public Health
410 Capitol Ave., MS# 12APP
Hartford, CT 06134

Delaware

Delaware Board of Examiners of Psychology
861 Silver Lake Blvd.
Cannon Bldg., Ste. 203
Dover, DE 19904
dpr.delaware.gov/boards/psychology

District of Columbia

District of Columbia Board of Psychology
825 N. Capitol St. NE, Ste. 2224
Washington, DC 20002

Florida

Florida Board of Psychology
4052 Bald Cypress Way, Bin #C05
Tallahassee, FL 32399

Georgia

Georgia State Board of Examiners of Psychologists
237 Coliseum Dr.
Macon, GA 31217
http://sos.georgia.gov/plb/psych

Hawaii

Hawaii Board of Psychology
Department of Commerce and Consumer Affairs
Honolulu, HI 96801
www.hawaii.gov/dcca/areas/pvl/boards/psychology

Idaho

Idaho State Board of Psychologist Examiners
Bureau of Occupational Licenses
1109 Main St., Ste. 220
Boise, ID 83702
http://ibol.idaho.gov/psy.htm

Illinois

Illinois Clinical Psychologists Licensing and Disciplinary
    Committee
Division of Professional Regulation
320 W. Washington St., 3rd Fl.
Springfield, IL 62786
www.idfpr.com/dpr/WHO/psych.asp

Indiana

Indiana State Psychology Board
Professional Licensing Agency
Attn: Indiana State Board of Dentistry
402 W. Washington St., Ste. W066
Indianapolis, IN 46204
www.in.gov/pla/bandc/ispb

Iowa

Iowa Board of Psychology Examiners
Department of Public Health
321 E. 12th St.
Lucas State Office Bldg., 5th Fl.
Des Moines, IA 50319

Kansas

Kansas Behavioral Sciences Regulatory Board
712 S. Kansas Ave.
Topeka, KS 66603
www.ksbsrb.org/psychologists.html

Kentucky

Kentucky State Board of Examiners of Psychology
P.O. Box 1360
Frankfort, KY 40602
http://finance.ky.gov/ourcabinet/caboff/OAS/op/psychbd

Louisiana

Louisiana State Board of Examiners of Psychologists
8280 YMCA Plaza Dr.
One Oak Square, Bldg. 8-B
Baton Rouge, LA 70810
www.lsbep.org

Maine

Maine Board of Examiners of Psychologists
35 State House Station
Augusta, ME 04333

Maryland

Maryland Board of Examiners of Psychologists
4201 Patterson Ave.
Baltimore, MD 21215
www.dhmh.state.md.us/html/proflicm.htm

Massachusetts

Massachusetts Board of Registration of Psychologists
Division of Registration
239 Causeway St.
Boston, MA 02114

Michigan

Michigan Board of Psychology
P.O. Box 30670
Lansing, MI 48909
www.michigan.gov/mdch

Minnesota

Minnesota Board of Psychology
2829 University Ave. SE, Ste. 320
St. Paul, MN 55414

Mississippi

Mississippi Board of Psychology
419 E. Broadway
Yazoo City, MS 13769

Missouri

Missouri State Committee of Psychologists
3605 Missouri Blvd.
Jefferson City, MO 65109
www.pr.mo.gov/psychologists.asp

Montana

Montana Board of Psychologists
301 S. Park Ave., Rm. 430
Helena, MT 59620
http://mt.gov/dli/bsd/license/bsd_boards/psy_board/board_page.asp

Nebraska

Nebraska Board of Psychologists
301 Centennial Mall South, 3rd Fl.
Lincoln, NE 68509
www.hhs.state.ne.us/crl/mhcs/psych/psych.htm

Nevada

State of Nevada Board of Psychological Examiners
P.O. Box 2286
Reno, NV 89505

New Hampshire

New Hampshire Board of Mental Health Practice
49 Donovan St.
Concord, NH 03301
www.nh.gov/mhpb

New Jersey

New Jersey State Board of Psychological Examiners
P.O. Box 45017
Newark, NJ 07101
www.state.nj.us/lps/ca/medical/psycho.htm

New Mexico

New Mexico Board of Psychologist Examiners
2550 Cerrillos Rd.
Santa Fe, NM 87505
www.rld.state.nm.us/Psychology

New York

New York State Board for Psychology
State Education Department, Office of the Professions
89 Washington Ave., 2nd Fl., East Wing
Albany, NY 12234
www.op.nysed.gov/psych

North Carolina

North Carolina Psychology Board
895 State Farm Rd., Ste. 101
Boone, NC 28607
www.ncpsychologyboard.org

North Dakota

North Dakota State Board of Psychologist Examiners
P.O. Box 7458
Bismarck, ND 58507

Ohio

Ohio State Board of Psychology
77 S. High St., Ste. 1830
Columbus, OH 43215
http://psychology.ohio.gov

Oklahoma

Oklahoma State Board of Examiners of Psychologists
201 Northeast 38th Terr., Ste. 3
Oklahoma City, OK 73105

Oregon

Oregon State Board of Psychologist Examiners
3218 Pringle Rd. SE, Ste. 130
Salem, OR 97302
www.obpe.state.or.us

Pennsylvania

Pennsylvania State Board of Psychology
2601 N. 3rd St.
Harrisburg, PA 17110
www.dos.state.pa.us/bpoa/cwp

Rhode Island

Rhode Island Board of Psychology
Office of Health Professionals Regulations
3 Capitol Hill, Rm. 104
Providence, RI 02908
www.health.ri.gov/hsr/professions/psych.php

South Carolina

South Carolina Board of Examiners in Psychology
P.O. Box 11329
Columbia, SC 29211
www.llr.state.sc.us/POL/Psychology

South Dakota

South Dakota Board of Examiners of Psychologists
135 E. Illinois, Ste. 214
Spearfish, SD 57783
www.state.sd.us/dhs/boards/psychologists/psych-ho.htm

Tennessee

Tennessee Board of Examiners in Psychology
425 5th Ave. N, 1st Fl.
Cordell Hull Bldg.
Nashville, TN 37243
www2.state.tn.us/health/Boards/Psychology

Texas

Texas State Board of Examiners of Psychologists
333 Guadelupe, Tower 2, Rm. 450
Austin, TX 78701
www.tsbep.state.tx.us

Utah

Utah Psychologist Licensing Board
Division of Occupational and Professional Licensing
160 E. 300 S, Box 146741
Salt Lake City, UT 84114
www.dopl.utah.gov/licensing/psychologist.html

Vermont

Vermont Board of Psychological Examiners
Office of Professional Regulation
26 Terrace St.
Montpelier, VT 05609
www.vtprofessionals.org/opr1/psychologists

Virgin Islands

Virgin Islands
Executive Secretary to Medical Boards
Office of the Commissioner
Roy L. Schneider Hospital
St. Thomas, VI 00801

Virginia

Virginia Board of Psychology
6603 W. Broad St., 5th Fl.
Richmond, VA 23230
www.dhp.state.va.us/psychology

Washington

Washington State Examining Board of Psychology
Dept. of Health
P.O. Box 47869
Olympia, WA 98504
https://fortress.wa.gov/doh/hpqa1/hps7/psychology/default.htm

West Virginia

West Virginia Board of Examiners of Psychologists
P.O. Box 3955
Charleston, WV 25339

Wisconsin

Wisconsin Psychology Examining Board
Dept. of Regulation and Licensing
Bureau of Health Service Professions
Madison, WI 53708

Wyoming

Wyoming State Board of Psychology
2020 Carey Ave., Ste. 201
Cheyenne, WV 82002
http://plboards.state.wy.us/Psychology/index.asp

Canada

Alberta

College of Alberta Psychologists
10123-99 St., 2100 Sunlife Pl.
Edmonton, AB T5J 3H1
www.cap.ab.ca

British Columbia

College of Psychologists of British Columbia
1755 W. Broadway, Ste. 404
Vancouver, BC V6J 4S5

Labrador

(*See* Newfoundland)

Manitoba

Psychological Association of Manitoba
162-2025 Corydon Ave., #253
Winnipeg, MB R3P 0N5

New Brunswick

College of Psychologists of New Brunswick
238 St. George St., Ste. 5
Moncton, NB E1C 1V9
www.cpnb.ca
www.cpnb.ca/french

Newfoundland and Labrador

Newfoundland and Labrador Board of Examiners in Psychology
    (NFPB)
P.O. Box 5666, Station C
St. John's, NF A1C 5W8
www.nbep.info

Nova Scotia

Nova Scotia Board of Examiners in Psychology
Halifax Professional Centre, Ste. 455
5991 Spring Garden Rd.
Halifax, NS B3H 1Y6
www.nsbep.org

Ontario

College of Psychologists of Ontario
L'Ordre des Psychologues de L'Ontario
110 Eglinton Ave. W, Ste. 500
Toronto, ON M4R 1A3
www.cpo.on.ca

Prince Edward Island

Psychologists Registration Board
Department of Psychology
University of Prince Edward Island
Charlottetown, PE C1A 4P3

Quebec

Ordre des Psychologues du Quebec
1100, rue Beaumont #510
Mont-Royal, QC H3P 3H5
www.ordrepsy.qc.ca

Saskatchewan

Saskatchewan College of Psychologists
348 Albert St.
Regina, SK S4R 2N2
www.skcp.ca

Further Reading

The following list represents just a sample of the many titles available for students of psychology.

American Psychological Association. *Getting In: A Step-by-Step Plan for Gaining Admission to Graduate School in Psychology.* Washington, D.C.: American Psychological Association, 2007.

American Psychological Association. *Graduate Study in Psychology,* 2007 ed. Washington, D.C.: American Psychological Association, 2007.

Aronson, Elliot. *Social Psychology,* 6th ed. Upper Saddle River, N.J.: Prentice Hall, 2006.

Attix, Deborah K., and Kathleen A. Welsh-Bohmer. *Geriatric Neuropsychology: Assessment and Intervention.* New York: Guilford Press, 2005.

Bersoff, Donald N. *Ethical Conflicts in Psychology,* 3rd ed. Washington, D.C.: American Psychological Association, 2003.

Bieling, Peter J. et al. *Cognitive-Behavioral Therapy in Groups*. New York: Guilford Press, 2006.

Blaine, Bruce E. *Understanding the Psychology of Diversity*. Thousand Oaks, Calif.: Sage Publications, 2007.

Brannon, Linda, and Jesse Feist. *Health Psychology: An Introduction to Behavior and Health*, 6th ed. Boston: Wadsworth Publishing, 2006.

Brown, Steven D., and Robert W. Lent, eds. *Handbook of Counseling Psychology*, 4th ed. New York: Wiley, 2008.

Buskist, William, and Caroline Burke. *Preparing for Graduate Study in Psychology: 101 Questions and Answers*, 2nd ed. New York: Wiley-Blackwell, 2006.

Carlson, Neil R. *Foundations of Physiological Psychology*, 7th ed. Boston: Allyn and Bacon, 2007.

Cascio, Wayne F., and Herman Aquinis. *Applied Psychology in Human Resource Management*, 6th ed. Upper Saddle River, N.J.: Prentice-Hall, 2004.

Cone, John D., and Sharon L. Foster. *Dissertations and Theses from Start to Finish: Psychology and Related Fields*, 2nd ed. Washington, D.C.: American Psychological Association, 2006.

Frisby, Craig, and Cecil R. Reynolds. *Comprehensive Handbook of Multicultural School Psychology*. New York: Wiley, 2005.

Furr, R. Michael, and Verne R. Bacharach. *Psychometrics: An Introduction*. Thousand Oaks, Calif: Sage Publications, 2007.

Gatchel, Robert J., and Mark S. Oordt. *Clinical Health Psychology and Primary Care: Practical Advice and Clinical Guidance for Successful Collaboration*. Washington, D.C.: American Psychological Association, 2003.

Hill, Clara E. *Helping Skills: Facilitating Exploration, Insight, and Action*, 2nd ed. Washington, D.C.: American Psychological Association, 2004.

Hyer, Lee, and Robert C. Intrieri, eds. *Geropsychological Interventions in Long-Term Care*. New York: Springer, 2006.

Jacob, Susan, and Timothy S. Hartshorne. *Ethics and Law for School Psychologists*, 5th ed. New York: Wiley, 2006.

Kring, Ann M. et al. *Abnormal Psychology*, 10th ed. New York: Wiley, 2006.

Landy, Frank L., and Jeffrey M. Conte. *Work in the 21st Century: An Introduction to Industrial and Organizational Psychology*, 2nd ed. Upper Saddle River, N.J.: Prentice-Hall, 2006.

Larsen, Randy J., and David M. Buss. *Personality Psychology: Domains of Knowledge About Human Nature*, 3rd ed. New York: McGraw-Hill, 2006.

Lefkowitz, Joel. *Ethics and Values in Industrial-Organizational Psychology*. Mahwah, N.J.: Lawrence Erlbaum, 2003.

Lowman, Rodney L. et al., eds. *The Ethical Practice of Psychology in Organizations*, 2nd ed. Washington, D.C.: American Psychological Association, 2006.

MacLin, M. Kimberly, and Robert L. Solso. *Experimental Psychology: A Case Approach*, 8th ed. Boston: Allyn and Bacon, 2007.

Melton, Gary B. et al. *Psychological Evaluations for the Courts: A Handbook for Mental Health Professionals and Lawyers*, 3rd ed. New York: Guilford Press, 2007.

Merrell, Kenneth W. *School Psychology for the 21st Century: Foundations and Practices*. New York: Guilford Press, 2006.

Millon, Theodore et al. *Personality Disorders in Modern Life*, 2nd ed. New York: Wiley, 2004.

Myers, Anne, and Christine H. Hansen. *Experimental Psychology*, 6th ed. Boston: Wadsworth Publishing, 2005.

Osborne, Jason. *Best Practices in Quantitative Methods*. Charlotte, N.C.: Information Age Publishing, 2008.

Page, Andrew C., and Werner G. K. Stritzke. *Clinical Psychology for Trainees: Foundations of Science-Informed Practice.* Cambridge: Cambridge University Press, 2006.

Pope, Kenneth S., and Melba J.T. Vasquez. *Ethics in Psychological Counseling*. San Francisco: Jossey-Bass, 2007.

Roberts, Michael C. *Handbook of Pediatric Psychology*, 3rd ed. New York: Guilford Press, 2005.

Rosenzweig, Mark R. et al. *Biological Psychology: An Introduction to Behavioral and Cognitive Neuroscience*. Sunderland, Mass.: Sinauer Associates, Inc., 2004.

Roth, Anthony, and Peter Fonagy. *What Works for Whom?: A Critical Review of Psychotherapy Research*, 2nd ed. New York: Guilford Press, 2005.

Santrock, John W. *Educational Psychology*, 3rd ed. New York: McGraw-Hill, 2006.

Sexton, Thomas. *Handbook of Family Therapy: The Science and Practice of Working with Families and Couples.* New York: Routledge, 2003.

Shaffer, David R., and Katherine Kipp. *Developmental Psychology: Childhood and Adolescence*, 7th ed. Boston: Wadsworth Publishing, 2006.

Shiraev, Eric, and David Levy. *Cross-Cultural Psychology: Critical Thinking and Contemporary Applications*, 3rd ed. Boston: Allyn and Bacon, 2006.

Slater, Alan, and Gavin Bremner, eds. *An Introduction to Developmental Psychology*. New York: Wiley-Blackwell, 2003.

Slavin, Robert E. *Educational Psychology: Theory and Practice*, 8th ed. Boston: Allyn and Bacon, 2005.

Spirito, Anthony, and Anne E. Kazak. *Effective and Emerging Treatments in Pediatric Psychology*. New York: Oxford University Press, 2005.

Sternberg, Robert J. *Career Paths in Psychology: Where Your Degree Can Take You*, 2nd ed. Washington, D.C.: American Psychological Association, 2006.

Stout, Chris E., and Laurie Cope Grand. *Getting Started in Private Practice: The Complete Guide to Building Your Mental Health Practice*. New York: Wiley, 2004.

VandenBos, Gary R., ed. *APA Dictionary of Psychology*. Washington, D.C.: American Psychological Association, 2006.

Weinberg, Robert S., and Daniel Gould. *Foundations of Sport and Exercise Psychology*, 4th ed. Champaign, Ill.: Human Kinetics Publishers, 2004.

Weiner, Irving B., and Allen K. Hess, eds. *The Handbook of Forensic Psychology*, 3rd ed. New York: Wiley, 2005.

Wickens, Christopher D. et al. *Introduction to Human Factors Engineering*, 2nd ed. Upper Saddle River, N.J.: Prentice Hall, 2003.

Williams-Nickelson, Carol, and Mitchell J. Prinstein, eds. *Internships in Psychology: The APAGS Workbook for Writing Successful Applications and Finding the Right Match*, 2005–2006 edition. Washington, D.C.: American Psychological Association, 2005.

Wilmore, Jack et al. *Physiology of Sport and Exercise*, 4th ed. Champaign, Ill.: Human Kinetics Publishers, 2007.